# CAST IRON

## COOKBOOK

### DELICIOUS AND SIMPLE COMFORT FOOD

**JOANNA PRUESS**

**PHOTOGRAPHY BY BATTMAN**

**SKYHORSE PUBLISHING**

# CAST IRON

## COOKBOOK

Skyhorse Publishing books may be purchased in bulk at special discounts
for sales promotion, corporate gifts, fundraising, or educational purposes.
Special editions can also be created to specifiations. For details,
contact the Special Sales Department, Skyhorse Publishing, 307 W. 36th
Street, 11th Floor, New York, NY 10018 or info@skyhorsepublishing.com.

Please visit our website at www.skyhorsepublishing.com

Paperback ISBN: 978-1-62087-260-4

10 9 8 7 6

Library of Congress Cataloging-in-Publication Data

Pruess, Joanna.
The cast iron cookbook / by Joanna Pruess.
p. cm.
Includes bibliographical references and index.
ISBN 978-1-60239-803-0 (alk. paper)
1. Cookery. I. Title.
TX714.P82 2009
641.5--dc22
2009023196

All photography by Battman, except for istockphoto images on pages 115,
127, 155, 189, and 190; and shutterstock on page 214.

Printed in China

*To Bob:* For being such a willing partner in everything, including countless trips to the market, acting as a cheerleader when things got tough, and sitting down with seeming alacrity to several versions of the same dishes in this book...plus a lot more.

*To Mom:* Thanks for working with me to remember those recipes from so long ago.

And finally, *to Nicole, Ben, and Justin:* You are, as always, my source of pride and inspiration.

"One is considered fortunate nowadays if by chance one of these iron utensils is handed down to them from the second to the third generation. It is on account of these wonderful Cast Iron utensils that you have such fond recollections of the rich, juicy steaks and chops your grandmother used to serve."

— *Aunt Ellen*

## Luncheon and Other Nibbles

## Vegetables and Other Sides

## Main Courses

### POULTRY

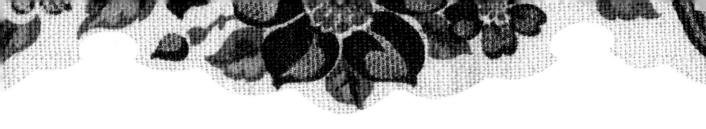

# Acknowledgments

**My profound thanks go to:**

First, Ann Treistman, my wonderful editor at Skyhorse Publishing, for another timely idea that evoked many happy memories, and for shepherding this project through with passion and wisdom;

Alan Batt (Battman) for your evocative photographs, easy disposition, and for going far beyond the call of duty to make the food look so real and tempting;

LeAnna Weller Smith, designer, for perfectly capturing the spirit of yesterday and today in this book and your generous, creative spirit;

David G. Smith—a.k.a. the Pan Man—for expert guidance in all matters relating to cast-iron cookware, including the history and care, and for loaning me archival materials;

Joel Schif—a prominent disciple of antique cast-iron cookware, and generous source of printed materials and information;

and to Jane Crosen for your copyediting and amusing, informative insights.

**Thanks to the following for your pots and palates, testing and other useful thoughts:**

Haejin Baek, Michael Berk, Sarah and Glenn Collins, Moira Crabtree, James Derek, Joe DiMaggio, Jr., Bobbie D'Angelo, Teresa Farney, Dianne Flamini, Lucio Galano and Louis Valantasis, Clara, Tony and the entire Grande family, Pam and John Harding, Elyse and John Harney, Deb Lape Lackowski, Lisa Ligas, Stephen and Sally Kahan, Carole and Winston Kulok, Sally Kofke and Gene Kofke, Geri and Kit Laybourne, Michael Pesce, Jane and Jack Quigley, Wendy Raymont, Janet Roth and Gary Rosenthal, Dick Saphir, Kathy and Tim Scheld, Anne Semmes, Roberta and Sandy Teller, Rick Waln and Debbie Lewis, and Judi Arnold of Dufour Pastry.

Finally, to the relatives, acquaintances, and friends over the years who left us recipes and happy food memories....

# Introduction

Compared with even a few years ago, life is more challenging. Whether earlier times were ever really kinder and gentler or just rose-colored dreams is debatable. But today, for whatever the reasons, many of us crave the comfort of the familiar in one form or another. That yearning is most obvious in our food choices: simplicity is the new sophistication and fussy fare seems dated.

Mac and cheese—just like mom's or dressed up—and succulent, fall-off-the-bone short ribs appear on bistro and fine-dining restaurant menus. Many homey dishes are served in the same cast-iron ramekins and casseroles in which they are cooked, even smugly sharing the table with Limoges porcelain.

Old-fashioned fare and cookware not only satisfy our hunger, on a primal level they reassure us by their link to the past...and seem so right for today.

## Old Is Newsworthy

Long before my great-grandmother simmered chicken paprikás in her Dutch oven, cast-iron cookware was appreciated. The Chinese began melting and forming the metal in the sixth century B.C. By the Middle Ages, tools and cookware that were cast in iron were so valuable they were listed as hereditary property in European estates; and in the fifteenth century, three-legged, dark gray iron cauldrons were common in hearths and fireplaces.

The pots arrived in the New World with the earliest European settlers. By the mid-nineteenth century, as Americans pushed beyond the Mississippi River across the Plains to the Old West, thousands of pioneers hitched oxen or mules to covered wagons. On the back of each chuck wagon, a thick-walled pot with a tight-fitting lid—the Dutch oven—was essential for cooking meals.

For the forty-niners who went to California during the Gold Rush, "Cooking was in black iron spiders (monumental cast iron frying pans on legs, originally designed for open hearth cooking and now pressed into service over the campfire) and Dutch ovens.

# "Drip-Drop" Roaster - An Old Fashioned Dutch Oven

THE very name, "Dutch Oven", makes you think of good, wholesome foods—juicy, tender meats and fowl, savory stews, wonderful roasts.

The modern housewife also prepares perfectly cooked food and at the same time is able to serve appetizing dishes with less worry and bother.

The Wagner "Drip-Drop" Roaster is a real old fashioned Dutch Oven with close fitting cover and the exclusive Wagner self-basting feature. The thorough distribution of the heat through its walls and bottom, the retention of all the moisture and juices during the cooking, and the "Drip-Drop" cover design insure evenly distributed basting.

The "Drip-Drop" Roaster is a typical Wagner Cast Iron De Luxe Utensil—carefully made, good looking, long wearing. Also made in Cast Aluminum. Your dealer should be able to supply you. Write for booklet.

**The Wagner Mfg. Co., Dept. 109, Sidney, Ohio**

Iron Deluxe        Cast Aluminum

"Meals were dished up with the sky as roof and the earth as dining table, around a fire of sage, twigs, or buffalo chips," writes Ann Chandonnet in *Gold Rush Grub: From Turpentine Stew to Hoochinoo* (University of Alaska Press, 2006).

David G. Smith, a preeminent cast-iron cookware historian (a.k.a. The Original Pan Man™), veteran collector, and co-founder of the Wagner and Griswold Society (www.wag-society.org), says that the first piece of cast-iron cookware made in the American Colonies was a small kettle cast in 1642, in Lynn, Massachusetts. Almost three centuries later, Wagner made a replica of that kettle.

The Hopewell Furnace, founded in 1771, and at its peak from 1820 to 1840, in Lancaster County, Pennsylvania's Amish country, also displays relics of cast-iron cookware produced from their blast furnace. It is interesting to note that they also made cannon balls for the Civil War.

While American stove companies were manufacturing what they called "stove furniture," or cookware, as accessories to their stoves from the early to late 1800s, historian Smith says that Griswold, of Erie, Pennsylvania, was the first company to specialize in the production of cast-iron cookware. An 1883 pocket-sized catalog details a limited line of cookware and hardware items and is recognized by most collectors as the starting date of Griswold cookware.

John Selden and Matthew Griswold originally began as fabricators of light hardware, including butt hinges, in 1865. After an 1885 reorganization, Selden was bought out and the firm was renamed Griswold Manufacturing Company. It remained under family control until 1957, when it was sold to the McGraw Edison Company. They, in turn, quickly sold off the cookware division to Wagner, resulting in Griswold's main competitor taking ownership of the name and trademarks.

The Wagner Manufacturing Company, founded by brothers Milton and Bernard Wagner, entered the cookware business in Sidney, Ohio, in 1891. In 1897, when an older brother, William, wanted to be a part of the family business, Wagner purchased the Sidney Hollow Ware foundry and installed William as manager. This arrangement lasted until 1903 when the Wagners sold Sidney Hollow Ware and brought William into the main firm.

Wagner's 1891 start-up date is supported by the fact that the General Housewares Corporation, another owner of Wagner, promoted a "Wagner's 1891" edition of cookware in 1991 to celebrate the company's one hundredth anniversary. However, because they couldn't locate a Wagner toy set to produce, they used a Griswold toy set to copy and marked the pieces "Wagner's 1891 Original."

Today, the proprietary metal formulas, trade secrets, and designs of Griswold and Wagner are owned by American Culinary Corporation, in Willoughby, Ohio. Both names remain synonymous with the most sought after and collected cast-iron cookware in America. As testimony to more than a century of dedication to unsurpassed quality and value, David G. Smith says sales of their cast-iron cookware have increased substantially.

Today, celebrated chefs and cooks like Emeril Lagasse, Tom Colicchio, Martha Stewart, and Paula Dean are among many who have joined the cast-iron band wagon as enthusiastic advocates.

## Why Cast-Iron Now?

As Teresa Farney, a friend and food editor of the Colorado Springs *Gazette*, puts it: "Do you really need to dish out hundreds of dollars for designer-label, high-end cookware when there's good old cast-iron around? Durable, functional and relatively inexpensive, cast-iron has so much going for it, it's a wonder more cooks don't use it. Maybe it's because cast-iron seems so old-fashioned compared to all the modern-looking $300-plus industrial cookware sets."

"Among its strengths is that the heavy metal retains heat well, which helps food cook quickly and evenly," Farney adds. The reason many people say that they buy a large black skillet in the first place is because they remember their mom or grandmother using it to make the best fried chicken. As a result of that weight—the cookware's only major draw-

back—the pans take longer to heat up than, say, stainless steel or aluminum, A quick rule of thumb is to allow 3 to 4 1/2 minutes, depending how hot the recipe says the pan should be. Since the handles are also made of metal, they also get hot, so a mitt is essential.

Cast-iron pots and pans are ideal for braising comfort-style dishes, like All-American Short Ribs, over low heat, as well as searing foods, like Turkey London Broil, over high heat on top of the stove and then finishing them in the oven. Throughout this book, I use every cooking technique from searing and sweating foods to simmering and frying—both deep fat and pan-frying—as well as caramelizing. The cookware can also go directly from the stove to the table.

Another friend, Marguerite Thomas, who writes for the Los Angeles Times International Syndicate, adds that the pans are wonderful on an induction cooktop, unlike those made of either copper or aluminum, which do not conduct (or "induce") magnetic energy from the cooktop and thus can't cause metal vessels to heat up. The only place cast-iron doesn't work is in a microwave.

As for what you can cook in cast-iron, my answer is just about everything. When I was learning to cook, I remember being told not to use cast-iron pans for tomatoes or other acidic foods because the metal can discolor or turn them bitter. However, over the years, and especially while testing the recipes in this book, my experience has been that if the pan is well-seasoned, this isn't a problem. That said, when cooking a lot of tomatoes, such as the sauce for Veracruz-Style Fish Fillets, where using cast-iron serves no real purpose in the recipe and/or the sauce is made separately anyway, I'd use a non-reactive skillet or pan, such as stainless steel. What I wouldn't do is store foods for a long time in the pots.

Once cast-iron pans are seasoned (see pages 24 to 25) and with minimal care—basically wiping and drying them over low heat, then spreading a thin layer of fat or even nonstick vegetable spray over them—they improve with use, developing that shiny surface that makes them so good for nonstick cooking without added fat. Their biggest foe is being ignored.

The pans are also an investment in the future and the health of our planet: Long after many expensive pots and pans (especially those with nonstick surfaces which can deteriorate over high heat) have been discarded, your cast-iron cookware will be serviceable and can be passed down to future generations. Even those that have been seriously abused can be cleaned and re-seasoned. There are tons of gray iron pots and pans in attics and at yard sales waiting to be adopted.

Incidentally, did you ever hear of anyone in your grandparents' generation with anemia? "Iron-poor blood" was pretty rare, since the tiny bit of iron that reacts with food supplies the essential nutrient to stave off that deficiency.

## Craving Foods from Yesteryear

As for why we are craving comfort food now, John DeLucie, the chef at The Waverly Inn in New York, writes in his recent memoir, *The Hunger* (HarperCollins, 2009), "After 9-11, New Yorkers were hankering for a nostalgic take on American dishes from a more innocent time. Nothing too fancy or 'chefy' as the partners liked to say," referring to how he made his mac and cheese exceptional

with truffles shaved on top.

"Real" foods—even if somewhat embellished—don't require mental gymnastics to appreciate. Their aromas and tastes can carry us back to more reassuring days shared with family and friends. Like the bite of tea-soaked madeleine that opened the floodgates to Marcel Proust's past, the smell of my mother's Chicken in a Pot as it roasted in the oven with an onion, tomatoes, and seasonings instantly transported me back to my childhood in Los Angeles. My re-creation of Tamale Pie, a favorite Tex-Mex casserole that a friend of my mom's made, with cornbread topping, chiles, spicy ground meat, and Cheddar cheese, also evoked happy memories.

While writing this book, I came across some bygone dishes and techniques that were unfamiliar to me, like the slowly roasted beef served by my husband's mother, Mary Lape (called "Mammy" because of Bob's early affection for the Li'l Abner comic strips). The entire Lape clan loves the dark, fork-tender meat and gravy thickened with flour and milk. For Nona's Meatloaf, Bobby D'Angelo's grandmother, Nora La Rose, made the ground beef mixture in the morning and then cooked the loaf with mushrooms and stock in the evening on top of the stove in her covered black skillet. It only took about 35 minutes. Like many back-to-basics foods, these dishes are made with inexpensive ingredients.

From the earliest days, Americans have used cast-iron skillets to bake desserts like Raspberry-Blackberry Crisp and Ginger-Spice-Topped Peach Cobbler because they are simple and the results are so rewarding. The same is true of the German Apple Pancake or *pfannkuchen* I used to make to the delight of my kids. As for Apple-Cherry Tarte Tatin, the renowned French upside-down fruit tart recalls my years in Paris.

## Connections to the Past and Future from Around the World

Today the tradition of America as a melting pot continues as new flavors and dishes are introduced with each wave of immigrants. Because of these newcomers, the media, and advances in transportation and technology, we have more diverse ingredients available and we are more open to new preparations. Dishes that once were difficult to re-create are being made with ease across our country.

Yet, for many of us, time remains the biggest challenge to preparing good meals, and I appreciate ways to cut corners without compromising the quality of the food. In some recipes, I use convenience items that didn't exist until fairly recently.

For example, the all-butter puff pastry I buy for the Provençal Onion, Tomato, and Olive Tart and for Tarte Tatin helps me to make these dishes more easily and better; and high-quality purchased pizza dough and sauce put the "easy" in Easy Chicago-Style Pizza.

Lest you think most cast-iron comfort foods take a lot of time, I suggest you try juicy Pan-Seared Pork Chops and Southern Fried Catfish for effortless, satisfying main courses. Both use my seasoning mix, but ready-made blends work as well. Joe DiMaggio, Jr.'s amazingly simple Chocolate Omelet Soufflé is also not only quick to make, it's a decadently delicious dessert.

Through sharing recipes with old and new friends, I realize that we can derive comfort from unfamiliar dishes as well as those we already know, so long as they please our palates and don't seem like work to under-

stand. When I perceive a link to how foods of different cultures are woven into our collective palate, they become more exciting to me.

For example, Louisiana-born Anne Semmes's perfectly spiced Creole Jambalaya, with andouille, chicken, and shrimp-laced rice, connects to the Spanish Paella I learned to make in Paris (from a Portuguese cook). Seoul-born Haejin Baek's Korean Short Ribs, flavored with soy, mirin, ginger, and garlic, and my bourbon-laced All-American Short Ribs are bonded by the same slow braising needed to tame the tough, meaty ribs into succulent, tender morsels.

Stuffed Peppers with Moroccan Lamb, scented with toasted almonds, minced prunes, cumin, and ginger and bound with couscous rather than rice, are seasoned differently from versions I knew in the past; so

is Nona's Meatloaf, in which the beef is mixed with milk-soaked bread, grated onion, and Parmesan cheese with no tomatoes or garlic. But dishes like these are homey and nurturing in tough times. I've also included Posole, a simple stew made with hominy, corn, and shrimp from the Native Americans of our Southwest.

Because food is dynamic and evolves, some dishes in this book are best described as contemporary. Hopefully you will find them satisfying, as well. Among my favorites are Panko-Macadamia-Crusted Salmon with Corn, Pepper, and Scallion Salsa; Steak 'n' Stout with Glazed Onions; and Sweet Potato Röstis.

Vegetable lovers (and even those who aren't) will find cooking in cast-iron coaxes flavors that are unachievable and more appealing than those resulting from any other cooking methods. Try Oven-Roasted

Asparagus with Macadamia Nuts or Brussels Sprouts with Bacon and Pistachios.

## A Return to Home Cooking

Finally, if the economy has a bright side, it's that this austere climate has brought people back to their kitchens and dining tables. Today we are participating more in our food choices and once again entertaining friends and family at home, often in more relaxed settings. And "the more people cook, the healthier they are," says Michael Pollan, the award-winning author of *In Defense of Food* (Penguin Press, 2009).

I believe many of us want to recapture a sense of community and sharing that may have been lost. Cast-iron cooking is both a simple and rewarding way to start, as I hope you discover in this book.

—Joanna Pruess, 2009

# Everybody Wants Waffles!

Madam, take a vote of your table some morning. See how many of your folks want waffles—
Dainty, crisp, golden brown waffles, smothered with maple syrup —the kind that melt in your mouth.
Every one of the family will raise their hand. They will be more than delighted with this kind of meal.
So let them feast on waffles for breakfast to-morrow and you'll add to your fame as a good cook.

# Griswold's Waffle Iron

### "Makes Waffles at Their Best"

Waffles are just as easy to cook as pancakes. Just as economical, too.

They are so simple to make, you haven't the slightest reason for doing without.

Follow any waffle recipe you wish, it makes no difference. The Griswold Iron will bake them to a delicate, crisp, golden brown.

It will bake them uniform throughout, and the flavor will be so delightful you never can forget it.

But be sure you use the Griswold Waffle Iron—the iron with extra thick pans, the iron that insures success.

The "Griswold" patent ball socket allows you to turn the waffles without lifting the pan—and extended grooved base plate catches all drops of grease or batter that overrun. Ventilated and insulated handles prevent burnt fingers.

Sold by dealers everywhere. If, for any reason, your dealer isn't supplied, write us and we'll tell you where you can get this perfect waffle iron. In all sizes for family use, from 95 cents up.

### Waffle Recipes—Free

Send postal for free booklet. It contains some old Southern Waffle Recipes and an article written by Miss Janet McKenzie Hill of the Boston Cooking School.

THE GRISWOLD MANUFACTURING CO., 1055 West Twelfth St., Erie, Pa.

We were thinking of You --- When we
"PRE-SEASONED"
GRISWOLD Cast Iron Cooking Ware

THE task of burning-off, scouring, greasing and breaking-in iron ware was a nuisance and too much hard work. We desired to make it easier for you to use Griswold iron utensils. Now we offer the ware "Pre-Seasoned" for immediate use in the home. It is the greatest improvement offered the housew... ...y years for her ease and convenience in cooking. You see, the laborious treatme... ...d" the utensils is eliminated. All you do, simply wash in warm soapy wat... ...and the utensil is ready for use. The "Pre-Seasoned" feature is a gr... ...here welcome it.

With ... ...designs, and sterling craftmanship, ... ...Seasoned' Iron Ware—Good

...king Utensil Lines

...of self-basting Dutch

...s and chicken f... ...on or without ...the

Aunt Ellen's
...LICIOUS
...H OVEN
...HES

CHEAPER C...
OF MEAT
AND HOW TO PREPARE TH...

GRISWOLD

HOME COMFORT

LAN-EASY FRI...

# Cleaning & Seasoning Cast-Iron Cookware

By David G. Smith, a.k.a. The Pan Man™

With proper care, your iron cookware will last forever and will require very little maintenance. If you have acquired a brand new pan, the manufacturer may have stated that it is "pre-seasoned." In most cases, this pre-seasoning is temporary. You will need to build up that seasoned surface. In this brief tutorial, I'll explain how to clean old pans, including rusted pans; how to season pans; and general cleaning and maintenance.

## Initial Cleaning

CAUTION: Wear rubber gloves and eye protection while doing this!

Let's begin with an old piece of cast iron that is dirty, cruddy with burned-on food residue, and perhaps also slightly rusted. To initiate the cleaning process, begin by spraying the pan with oven cleaner, putting it in a plastic bag, and tying it shut. The bag will keep the oven cleaner from drying out, so it will continue to work. Leave the pan as it is for two or three days.

Then remove it from the bag, and scrub it with a brush—my favorite is a brass brush I found at the automotive counter of my local hardware store. This brush is marketed for cleaning white wall tires. It is just the right size for doing pans. You can also find brass brushes at the grocery store in the kitchenware aisle or even in your drugstore.

If all the burned on grease doesn't come off on this first try, repeat the process with the bag and the oven cleaner, concentrating the cleaner to the troublesome areas.

For cleaning many pieces at one time, you can prepare a soaking solution of one and a half gallons of water to one (18-ounce) can of lye in a plastic container. Lye, like oven cleaner, is very caustic and will burn you. Always wear rubber gloves.

Mix enough solution in the plastic container to cover the items to be cleaned. Leave the pieces in the soak for about five days; then scrub the pieces. You can use the lye mixture several times. (Be careful not to use oven cleaner or lye on aluminum, finished wooden handles, pans with porcelain or enameled finishes as they will be destroyed.)

Finish the cleaning process as above.

I **DO NOT** recommend the following methods of cleaning:

• **Open fire:** The intense heat can severely warp or even crack the piece.

• **Self-cleaning oven:** Although this doesn't hold as great a risk as throwing it in a fire, the intense heat of a self-cleaning oven can warp a skillet. There is also a risk of cracking the piece.

• **Sandblasting:** This is the cardinal sin for collectors. Sandblasting destroys the patina making the piece a dull gray color. Most collectors will not buy a piece that has been sandblasted.

## To Remove Rust

Buff the pan with a fine wire wheel of an electric drill. Crusted rust can then be dissolved by soaking the piece in a solution of equal amounts of white vinegar and water for a few hours. Don't leave it longer than overnight without checking it. This solution will eventually eat the iron!

It is now important to neutralize and stop the action of the vinegar so it won't continue to attack the iron. To do this, apply the oven cleaner again and let the piece soak overnight. You can also soak the piece overnight in an alkaline solution, such as washing soda, which is available in the cleaning department of most supermarkets and some hardware stores. Scrub the piece in dish detergent and hot water before seasoning.

## Seasoning

After removing the burned-on grease, you are ready to season the piece. Preheat the oven to 125°F. This removes any moisture in the oven which could condense on the cold skillet, leaving a very fine gold or rust color.

Heat the piece in the preheated oven for about 15 minutes or until hot. Carefully remove the hot pan and apply shortening all over it. I prefer solid Crisco, but you can also use lard or bacon grease. I don't recommend oil, but it can be used. Solid Crisco will flow right on. Of course, you have to use a hot pad or rag to hold them.

Return the pots to the oven right side up and raise the temperature to 225°F. Leave them in the oven for 30 minutes, then remove and wipe off any pooled shortening, leaving the piece still shining wet. The timing is important here because if you leave them in the oven too long, the shortening begins to thicken.

Return the pieces to the oven for another 30 minutes. Remove and let them cool down for 10 to 15 minutes or until they are very warm but not too hot to work with, then wipe them to a dull shine. If the shiny surface resists wiping, the pan is too cool. The initial seasoning should be accomplished at this point. However, typical of cast-iron cookware, the more you use it (and don't abuse it) the better it will be.

It is generally recommended that you cook fatty foods in the pan the first few times you use it as this adds to the seasoning process. This goes for new pre-seasoned pans as well.

Before adding any fat to the pan when you're cooking, heat the pan for 3 1/2 to 4 minutes over medium to high, until hot but not smoking, unless otherwise indicated in the recipe.

## Routine Care

CAUTION: DO NOT put cold water in a hot pan! Cold water will crack a hot pan!

DO NOT use detergent to clean a cast-iron pan after cooking with it. That will destroy the seasoning. Instead, put hot water in the pan and bring it to a boil. Let the pan soak for several minutes, then wipe it out with a paper towel. If something sticks, scrape it with a spoon to dislodge it. Do not use a Brillo or other abrasive metal pads to scour the pan as they cut into the seasoned surface.

Next, reheat the pan and apply a fine coating of shortening, oil, or even a nonstick spray, such as Pam. It should just wet the surface and shouldn't run. Wipe off enough of the heated oil to leave the pan with a dull shine. As you use the piece and continue with this maintenance seasoning process, your pan will develop a nice black patina and a stick free surface.

If you follow these suggestions, you'll be able to pass on your favorite skillets to your children and grandchildren! I know they last—I've been collecting cast iron for more than thirty years and currently buy and sell at www.panman.com. In addition, I coauthored *The Book of Griswold & Wagner* and *The Book of Wagner & Griswold.*

# The AUNT ELLEN BOOKLET on WATERLESS COOKING

# DELICIOUS DUTCH OVEN DISHES

## With Recipes for Cooking the Less Expensive and Less Known Cuts of Meat

*Aunt Ellen's Directions for*
Roasting, Baking, Frying
and Stewing

"The Griswold Tite-Top Dutch Oven has been tested and approved by the Good Housekeeping Institute, the Pratt Institute, Tribune Institute, and other similar organizations."

Look for this star and seal. It is the sign of approval by the Good Housekeeping Institute conducted by Good Housekeeping Magazine.

# DELICIOUS CRISP AND BROWN WAFFLES

STAMBAUGH-THOMPSON Co.
House Furnishing Department
YOUNGSTOWN, OHIO

# GRISWOLDS AMERICAN WAFFLE IRONS

# FIFTY FAMOUS RECIPES BY AUNT ELLEN

OUT of a savory kitchen come these recipes—for cakes, puddings, cookies, doughnuts, ices, relishes, corn pones, pot roasts, barbecued meats. You will find them in no other recipe book of any sort.

There's a strange mustard gravy. There are confection waffles with chopped pecans, dripping with velvety hard sauce. There's chicken like some new white-meat fowl you never tasted before.

There's a lemon pie that makes its two top layers by itself! And there are little cakes full of surprises . . . preserves you like to serve in clear crystal . . . a cake icing that is moist and mallowy, and loops down upon the cake as you spoon it from the platter till you spread it roughly, like a fondant paste.

Have this on devil's food some day with your Mexican Meat Roll dinner. Baked bananas, too, and Delmonico potatoes, pickle relish—marshmallow pudding for the cake, and then coffee. At some occasional guest time, have fried chicken Louisiane, riced potatoes, green peppers stuffed with tomatoes, butter cakes, to eat with French melange—and for dessert green apple sauce with brown sugar cookies. Many other delightful menus will suggest themselves to you as you read.

Aunt Ellen's DELICIOUS MEAT DISHES

# About *Aunt Ellen*

❦ *Write "Aunt Ellen," at the Griswold Kitchen, any time you want advice about recipes, or want more recipes, or want to know more about "Waterless Cooking" or Griswold "Waterless Utensils." The Aunt Ellen service is always free. The Griswold Mfg. Company, Erie, Pa.*

Aunt Ellen was "born" in the 1920s, when Miss M. Etta Moses began fielding letters received at the Griswold Manufacturing Company about the use and care of the brand's cookware utensils.

She soon began offering recipes and advice on cooking with cast-iron, under the pen name "Aunt Ellen." Griswold's commercial cookware lines were founded around that time, and after World War II included complete kitchenware packages, so there was a need for a woman's voice in their ranks.

Aunt Ellen became so well-known that stacks of mail came across her desk every day for her hints and advice. And continued to do so for twenty-five years.

Miss M. Etta Moses died in 1948, after more than fifty years as a Griswold employee.

Her recipes and advice, included throughout this book, are as helpful and as much fun to read as they were nearly a century ago.

# GRISWOLD and WAGNER WARE

# CAST IRON

## COOKBOOK

{ *Luncheon & Other Nibbles* }

*When I was growing up, my mother made scrumptious macaroni and cheese with creamy sauce, sautéed onions, paprika, and loads of Tillamook or sharp Cheddar cheese. My siblings and I loved it, especially the crunchy-cheesy topping. Mom baked the casserole in the cast-iron Dutch oven she received as a wedding present. I prefer to use a 10-inch skillet.*

*When I added bacon to the filling and Parmesan cheese and panko bread crumbs to the topping, my kids and friends attacked that mac with a vengeance, thus it took on the name "macattacaroni." My favorite pasta for this is cellentani, a tubular cork-screw shape that has a ridged surface.*

# Mom's Mac and Cheese with Bacon

*Serves 8*

Preheat your oven to 350°F. Bring a large pot of salted water to a boil. Add the pasta and cook until al dente, about 10 minutes; drain and set aside.

Meanwhile, put the bacon in a 10-inch Dutch oven or skillet and cook it over medium heat for 3 minutes or until a little bacon fat covers the bottom of the pan. Stir in the onions and continue to cook until they are golden and the bacon is cooked through, about 4 minutes more, stirring frequently.

Add enough of the butter so you have 3 tablespoons of fat in the pan. When it has melted, stir in the flour and cook until lightly colored, about 3 minutes, stirring constantly. Whisk in the milk and bring to a boil, stirring until smooth. Reduce the heat and simmer for 10 minutes or until the sauce thickens, stirring occasionally. Add 3 cups of the cheese and stir until

½ pound uncooked elbow macaroni, cellentani, or other tubular pasta

¼ pound thick-sliced lean bacon, cut crosswise into ½-inch pieces

1 medium yellow onion, peeled and diced

1 to 2 tablespoons unsalted butter

3 tablespoons unbleached all-purpose flour

3 ¼ cups whole milk

4 cups (1 pound) shredded sharp Cheddar cheese

1 teaspoon salt or to taste

1 teaspoon paprika

Freshly ground black pepper

½ cup grated Parmigiano-Reggiano cheese

⅓ cup panko bread crumbs, found in the Asian food section of supermarkets

*Note:* Try any of the following mac and cheese additions: cooked chunks of kielbasa, chorizo, or any sausage; cooked chunks of lobster; diced canned or chopped sun-dried tomatoes; a small white truffle thinly shaved and/or white truffle oil; and, of course, canned tuna...a.k.a. Tuna Casserole!

it has melted. Stir the macaroni and season with paprika, salt, and pepper to taste.

Combine the remaining cup of Cheddar, the Parmigiano-Reggiano, and panko crumbs in a bowl. Spoon the mixture over the macaroni and bake for 30 minutes or until the top is golden brown. If it is not browned enough, turn the broiler on and cook for 3 to 4 minutes longer, watching carefully that it doesn't burn. Remove the casserole and cool for 5 minutes before serving.

# Aunt Ellen's Delicious Kitchen Tested Dishes

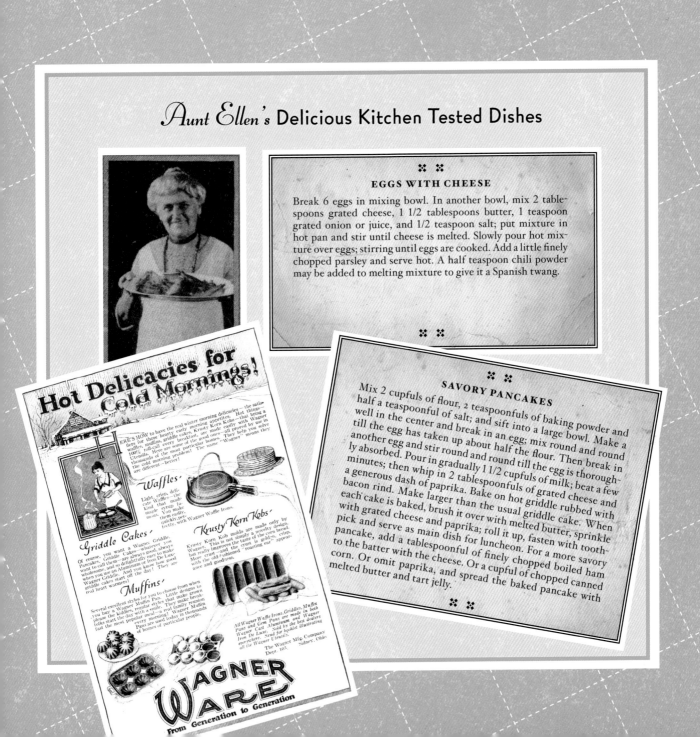

## EGGS WITH CHEESE

Break 6 eggs in mixing bowl. In another bowl, mix 2 table-spoons grated cheese, 1 1/2 tablespoons butter, 1 teaspoon grated onion or juice, and 1/2 teaspoon salt; put mixture in hot pan and stir until cheese is melted. Slowly pour hot mixture over eggs; stirring until eggs are cooked. Add a little finely chopped parsley and serve hot. A half teaspoon chili powder may be added to melting mixture to give it a Spanish twang.

## SAVORY PANCAKES

Mix 2 cupfuls of flour, 2 teaspoonfuls of baking powder and half a teaspoonful of salt; and sift into a large bowl. Make a well in the center and break in an egg; mix round and round till the egg has taken up about half the flour. Then break in another egg and stir round and round till the egg is thorough-ly absorbed. Pour in gradually 1 1/2 cupfuls of milk; beat a few minutes; then whip in 2 tablespoonfuls of grated cheese and a generous dash of paprika. Bake on hot griddle rubbed with bacon rind. Make larger than the usual griddle cake. When each cake is baked, brush it over with melted butter, sprinkle with grated cheese and paprika; roll it up, fasten with tooth-pick and serve as main dish for luncheon. For a more savory pancake, add a tablespoonful of finely chopped boiled ham to the batter with the cheese. Or a cupful of chopped canned corn. Or omit paprika, and spread the baked pancake with melted butter and tart jelly.

# Provençal Onion, Tomato, and Olive Tart

## (Pissaladière)

### Serves 4 to 6

*Pissaladières are popular pizza-like snacks in the south of France. Some of the most delicious are made with puff pastry. Although my version isn't classic, friends love the generous tangle of sautéed onions, sun-dried tomatoes, olives, and minced anchovies baked with the flaky crust on top, like a Tarte Tatin (page 192), then flipped before serving. The thin layer of caramel accents the tangy onions and salty anchovies. The tart is best eaten soon after baking.*

1 (14-ounce) package all-butter puff pastry, defrosted according to package directions

¾ pound yellow onions, peeled, cut in half lengthwise and thinly sliced crosswise

2 tablespoons olive oil

2 tablespoons white balsamic vinegar

½ tablespoon herbes de Provence

½ teaspoon salt

Freshly ground black pepper

3 tablespoons sugar

1 ½ tablespoons water

⅔ cup (3 ounces) sun-dried tomatoes, blotted dry and thinly sliced

⅓ cup (2 ounces) pitted oil-cured black olives, chopped

4 to 5 canned anchovies, rinsed, blotted dry and roughly chopped

Preheat your oven to 425°F. Unfold the pastry and, using a circular pattern, cut it into an 11-inch round; lay the dough on a cutting board, cover with a towel, and refrigerate for 1 hour.

Meanwhile, heat a 10-inch cast-iron skillet over medium-high heat until hot but not smoking, 3 1/2 to 4 minutes. In a large bowl, combine the onions and oil; add them to skillet and sauté over medium-low heat until they are golden, about 15 minutes, stirring often. Pour in the vinegar, raise the heat to high, and boil until the vinegar evaporates, about 30 seconds, stirring often. Scrape the onions into a bowl, then stir in the herbes de Provence, salt, and a generous amount of pepper.

Wipe out the skillet and heat it over medium-high heat. Add the sugar and water and cook until the sugar melts and turns a rich amber brown, about 5 minutes, rotating the pan to coat it evenly. Remove the skillet from the heat and spoon the onions over the caramel; scatter the tomatoes, olives, and anchovies evenly over the onions and lay the puff pastry on top, tucking the edges into the pan. With a sharp knife, make four or five 1-inch cuts in the top.

Bake in the middle of the oven for 10 minutes; adjust the heat down to 350° and continue baking until the crust is puffed and golden, about 20 minutes. Remove and let it stand for 5 minutes. Run a knife around the edges of the pan to loosen the pastry, then place a 10-inch plate directly on the pissaladière and flip it out. Replace any ingredients that remain in the pan. With a serrated knife, cut the pissaladière into wedges and serve.

# My Favorite Deep-Dish Vegetarian Pizza

*Serves 4 as a main course*

*This substantial deep-dish pizza of broccoli, sun-dried tomatoes, olives, and artichoke hearts is topped with mozzarella and a final shower of fresh basil leaves. To me, this is comfort food. The cheese sprinkled over most of the ingredients prevents the ingredients from burning or drying out. Be sure to let the pizza rest once it comes from the oven; this way, the pizza will easily slide out of the skillet, and you won't burn your mouth.*

1 pound pizza dough, defrosted in the refrigerator, if frozen (see the recipe notes on page 42)

2 tablespoons olive oil

1 small yellow onion, peeled and thinly sliced crosswise

1 cup purchased Italian tomato pasta sauce

2 large cloves garlic, peeled and minced

2 cups small broccoli florets, cooked

½ cup (2 ounces) sun-dried tomatoes in oil, blotted on paper towels and thinly sliced

⅓ cup (2 ounces) pitted oil-cured olives, chopped

1 ½ teaspoons dried oregano, crushed

Pinch of red pepper flakes, crushed (optional)

2 cups (½ pound) shredded low-moisture mozzarella

1 (6.5-ounce) jar marinated and quartered artichoke hearts, drained and blotted on paper towels

2 tablespoons grated Parmigiano-Reggiano

2 tablespoons julienned fresh basil leaves

Remove the dough from the refrigerator about 1 hour before starting to prepare the pizza. Preheat your oven to 500°F and position the rack in the lower third of the oven.

Heat a 10-inch cast-iron skillet over medium-high heat until hot but not smoking, 3 1/2 to 4 minutes. Add 1 tablespoon of the oil and the onions and sauté until they are limp and golden brown, about 3 minutes; remove with a slotted spoon to a bowl. Wipe out the skillet and brush the bottom and sides with oil.

Work the dough into a disc about 12 inches in diameter, pressing from the center outwards with your fingertips and gently stretching it. Lay it in the skillet and gently push it up the sides, taking care not to tear it. If the dough extends over the edges, trim it even with the pan. The sauce will help hold it up.

Ladle on the sauce, spreading it with a spatula to within 1/2 inch of the edges; add the garlic, onion, broccoli, sun-dried tomatoes, and olives followed by the oregano, pepper flakes,

and finally the mozzarella. Bake for 15 minutes; then add the artichoke hearts, sprinkle on the cheese, adjust the heat down to 400°, and cook until the cheese is bubbling and golden brown, 8 to 10 minutes.

Remove the pizza from the oven and let cool for at least 15 minutes. Then, using a wide metal spatula, slide the pizza onto a cutting board. Sprinkle on the basil and, if desired, brush the crust with the remaining oil, then slice and serve.

# Easy Chicago-Style Pizza

*Serves 4 to 6*

*I love deep-dish pizzas because, for me, it's all about the filling. This classic pie includes sautéed onions, sausages, and mozzarella, but you can—and should—improvise. (My Favorite Deep-Dish Vegetarian Pizza is on page 38.) Purchased pizza dough and tomato sauce make this easy. Ask your favorite pizzeria if they'll sell you a ball of dough; many will. Supermarkets also sell fresh and frozen dough, but avoid those that say "multi-purpose dough for white bread" because they make an unappealingly soft crust. My favorite purchased tomato sauce for this pizza is puttanesca-style with olives, onions, and capers. You can assemble this pizza several hours ahead of time and keep it refrigerated until baking.*

1 pound pizza dough, defrosted in the refrigerator, if frozen

2+ tablespoons olive oil

1 medium yellow onion, peeled and thinly sliced crosswise

½ pound hot or sweet Italian sausages (according to taste), casings removed

1 cup purchased Italian tomato pasta sauce

2 large cloves garlic, peeled and minced

2 teaspoons dried oregano, crushed

Pinch of red pepper flakes, crushed (optional)

2 cups (½ pound) shredded low-moisture mozzarella

Remove the dough from the refrigerator about 1 hour before starting to prepare the pizza. Preheat your oven to 500°F and position the rack in the lower third of the oven. Line a large plate with paper towels.

Heat a 10-inch cast-iron skillet over medium-high heat until hot but not smoking, 3 1/2 to 4 minutes. Add 1 tablespoon of the oil and the onions to the pan and sauté until they are limp and golden brown, about 3 minutes; with a slotted spoon, remove them to the paper towel–lined plate.

Add the remaining oil and sausages to the skillet, breaking them into pieces with a wooden spatula; cook until the meat is no longer pink, about 4 minutes, stirring frequently. Remove the sausage to the plate with the onions. Wipe out the skillet and brush the bottom and sides with a little oil.

Work the dough into a disc about 12 inches in diameter, pressing from the center outwards with your fingertips and gently stretching it. Lay it in the skillet and gently push it up the sides, taking care not to tear it. If the dough extends over the edges, trim it even with the pan. The sauce will help hold it up.

Ladle the sauce evenly over the dough, leaving a 1/2-inch border at the outside. Add the sausage and onion followed by the garlic, oregano, pepper flakes, and finally the mozzarella. Transfer the skillet to the oven and bake for 15 minutes; adjust the heat down to 400° and continue cooking until the cheese is bubbling and golden brown, about 10 minutes more. Remove the pizza from the oven and cool for at least 15 minutes; then, using a wide metal spatula, slide the pizza onto a cutting board. If desired, brush the crust with a little oil, then slice and serve.

# Swiss Cheese and Apple Frittata

*Serves 4 to 5 as a first course or light main course*

When I first started making frittatas, they were usually with sautéed vegetables like zucchini and onions. But after developing the recipes for an article about the flat Italian omelets, I discovered numerous foods took well to the basic technique. For example, apples and cheese are often served together. I combined them with toasted almonds and onions into a savory appetizer or light main course. You can also cut a frittata into squares to serve as an hors d'oeuvre for 12 to 15 guests. In that case, you can make it ahead and serve it at room temperature.

5 large eggs

½ teaspoon water

1 teaspoon finely chopped tarragon leaves

½ teaspoon salt, or to taste

¼ teaspoon ground nutmeg

⅛ teaspoon white pepper

2 tablespoons unsalted butter

1 teaspoon canola or vegetable oil

1 medium yellow onion, peeled and chopped

2 medium Granny Smith or other tart green apples, peeled, cored, and chopped fairly fine

⅓ cup slivered almonds, toasted in a 350°F oven or toaster oven until lightly browned

1 cup (4 ounces) shredded Gruyère or other Swiss cheese

Chopped flat-leaf parsley, to garnish

In a large bowl, beat the eggs and water together. Stir in the tarragon, salt, nutmeg, and white pepper. Preheat your oven to 350°F.

Heat a 10-inch cast-iron skillet over medium-high heat until hot but not smoking, 3 1/2 to 4 minutes. Add 1 tablespoon of the butter, the oil, and chopped onion, and sauté until the onions are golden, 3 to 4 minutes, stirring occasionally. Add the apples and cook until limp, 3 to 4 minutes. Scrape them into the egg mixture, then add the slivered almonds and mix well.

Melt the remaining 1 tablespoon of butter over medium-high heat; pour in the egg mixture, shaking to distribute the ingredients evenly. Cook for 1 minute, then sprinkle on the cheese and adjust the heat to low. After 10 minutes, loosen the edges with a metal spatula, gradually working under the entire frittata. Shake the pan to be sure it is detached. Transfer the skillet to the oven and bake until the eggs are set, 4 to 5 minutes. Remove, cut into wedges, and serve with a little parsley on top.

# Croque Monsieur

*Serves 2*

In France, when the proverbial ham-and-cheese sandwich is grilled, it rises to new culinary heights and is called a Croque Monsieur. Some versions are dipped in egg before cooking, but I think my way is so easy and offers almost instant gratification. You can also make the sandwiches with sliced turkey or chicken from the deli. I like to turn the sandwiches a couple of times to get those appealing cross-hatch grill marks on the bread.

4 slices firm white bread

2 tablespoons softened unsalted butter

4 ounces thinly sliced Swiss cheese (4 slices), preferably Gruyère or other imported cheese

2 ounces thinly sliced boiled or baked ham (2 slices)

Dijon mustard

Heat a cast-iron grill pan or griddle over medium heat until hot but not smoking. Butter one side of each piece of bread. Lay the slices on a cutting board with the buttered sides down. Divide the cheese evenly among the four slices (you may have to fold the slices in half to fit the bread). Put ham on two slices, spread each with a generous teaspoon of Dijon mustard, and then put the remaining two cheese-covered slices on top.

Put the sandwiches in the grill pan and cook for 1 minute, pressing lightly with a spatula; then turn and cook the other side for 1 minute. Turn the sandwich back over, cook for 1 minute or until the toast is golden brown; turn again and cook until both sides are golden, rotating them about a quarter turn from where the original grill marks are to finish cooking and create those attractive cross-hatch grill marks. Remove the sandwiches from the grill, cut them into halves, and serve.

# Quesadillas Españolas

*Makes 8 triangles;*
*serves 4 as an hors d'oeuvre*
*or 1-2 for lunch*

*Quesadillas are typically Mexican or Southwestern American-style snacks made with white or whole wheat flour tortillas and melted cheese. (In Spanish, the word quesadilla means "little cheesy thing.") But once you've made a couple of quesadilla variations, you'll figure out many other possibilities. For example, these tasty triangles are filled with Spanish ingredients—Manchego cheese and Serrano ham—and topped with Spanish smoked paprika.*

2 (10-inch) flour tortillas

1 cup (4 ounces) shredded Manchego cheese

3 very thin slices dry-cured Serrano ham or prosciutto (1 ½ ounces)

½ tablespoon small capers, blotted dry

Olive oil

Pinch of sweet Pimentón de la Vera (see note)

Sprinkle half of the cheese evenly over one tortilla and cover with the ham. Sprinkle on the capers, then cover with the remaining cheese and second tortilla.

Heat a 10-inch cast-iron skillet over medium heat until hot but not smoking, 3 1/2 to 4 minutes; brush with a little oil. Put the filled quesadilla in the pan, brush the top with a little oil, and put a small skillet or pan on top and cook until the edges of the tortilla are browned, 2 to 3 minutes. With a wide spatula, flip the tortilla, and cook the other side until lightly browned, about 2 minutes. Remove the quesadilla, sprinkle on the Pimentón de la Vera, and let it stand for 1 minute; then cut into eighths with a pizza cutter or sharp knife, and serve.

*Note:* Spanish smoked paprika is known as Pimentón de la Vera. There are two varieties: sweet *(dulce)* and hot *(picante)*. It is made from dried peppers that are slowly smoked over an oak fire for several weeks to impart the characteristic smoky flavor to many authentic Spanish dishes.

*Here's another global approach to quesadillas: pan-fried tortillas filled with zesty Chinese-flavored pork (or turkey, if you prefer) topped with Jack cheese. While cheese isn't typical in Asian foods, I like this fusion of flavors.*

Heat a 10-inch cast-iron skillet over medium-high heat until hot but not smoking, 3 1/2 to 4 minutes, and brush with 2 teaspoons of oil. Add the pork or turkey and cook until it is no longer pink, breaking it into small pieces with a wooden spatula, about 5 minutes; stir in the cilantro, scallion, water chestnuts, hoisin, soy sauce, ginger, and chili oil. Scrape the mixture into a bowl and wipe out the skillet.

Heat the skillet over medium heat until hot but not smoking, 3 1/2 to 4 minutes; brush with a little oil. Lightly brush one side of the first tortilla with oil and place it oiled-side down in the skillet. Spoon the meat evenly on top of the tortilla; sprinkle on the cheese and top with the second tortilla, lightly brushing the top with oil. Place a small heavy skillet (or pan with a can of food in it) on the quesadilla and cook until nicely browned, 1 to 1 1/2 minutes, checking that it doesn't burn.

Turn the quesadilla and cook the other side until the cheese is melted and the tortilla is lightly browned, about 1 to 2 minutes more. Remove, cut into eighths with a pizza cutter or sharp knife, and serve.

# Asian Quesadillas

*Makes 8 triangles; serves 4 as an hors d'oeuvre or 1-2 for lunch*

Canola or vegetable oil

5 ounces ground pork or ground turkey

3 tablespoons finely chopped cilantro leaves

3 tablespoons finely chopped scallion + thinly sliced scallion greens, to garnish

3 canned water chestnuts, finely chopped

3 tablespoons hoisin sauce

1 ½ teaspoons soy sauce

1 teaspoon minced fresh ginger root

1 teaspoon hot chili oil

1 cup (4 ounces) shredded Monterey Jack or other mild cheese

2 (10-inch) flour tortillas

# Portobello Tuna Melt

*Serves 2*

*Portobello mushroom caps are a stand-in for the "bun" in this open-faced tuna melt. Cooked until barely tender, the mushrooms add a nutty, full flavor to this savory combination of tuna, provolone, and lightly dressed arugula salad for an easy, fast, and satisfying lunch or light dinner.*

4 tablespoons olive oil

1 (6-ounce) can imported solid light tuna in olive oil, drained and flaked

2 tablespoons mayonnaise

2 tablespoons each finely chopped celery, shallots, and flat-leaf parsley

2 teaspoons capers, chopped
2 portobello mushroom caps, about 5 inches in diameter, stems removed and wiped

Salt and freshly ground black pepper

1 teaspoon herbes de Provence or dried Italian herbs

2 slices (about 2 ounces) provolone cheese

2 cups baby arugula leaves or field greens

1 teaspoon balsamic vinegar

1 small tomato, thinly sliced, to garnish

Chopped flat-leaf parsley, to garnish

Turn your oven on to broil; position the rack close to the heat source. Heat a large cast-iron skillet over medium-high heat until hot but not smoking, 3 1/2 to 4 minutes, and brush with a little oil.

In a small bowl, blend the tuna, mayonnaise, celery, shallots, parsley, and capers.

Brush the mushroom caps with oil, place them in the skillet, stem-side down, and cook for 2 minutes. Brush the outside with a little more oil, turn them over, and turn off the heat. Brush the stem side with a little more oil, season with salt and pepper to taste, and sprinkle on the herbes de Provence or Italian herbs. Spoon the tuna into the caps, cover with provolone, and place the skillet under the broiler; cook until the cheese is bubbling, 2 to 3 minutes.

Meanwhile, toss the arugula with the remaining oil and balsamic vinegar, and season to taste with salt and pepper. Divide the salad between two plates. Remove the mushrooms from the oven and serve one on each plate. Garnish with a couple slices of tomato and a sprinkle of parsley, and serve.

# Sandwiches and Cold Meats

For parties, picnics, luncheons, or even a light, but fairly substantial meal, the sandwich is a great favorite since it offers a tempting and delicious medium for the serving of a countless variety of left-overs, cold meats, fruits, vegetables, and combinations. Any of the meat salads make choice sandwiches, and when delicately and temptingly served, will add to the reputation of the hostess.

All sandwiches should be so prepared that every particle is edible. The crust of the bread, while highly nutritious, is usually discarded for appearance sake, leaving the slices in squares, rectangles or triangles, and usually trimmed after the sandwich is completed. First trimmed to a full square, they may be cut across to form rectangles or smaller squares, or cut diagonally to form large or small triangles.

For plain sandwiches, when a considerable number must be prepared and the sandwiches small, the slices of bread should be not more than an eighth to a quarter inch in thickness, and are best if lightly buttered before trimming the crust.

Doubtless the most delicious sandwiches are those made with toasted white bread lightly buttered; however, it is quite a task to prepare these if any considerable quantity is required. For these, the bread should be sliced about half-inch thick, trimmed to a square and *quickly* toasted to a delicate golden brown on a *hot* toaster, care being taken not to leave the toast brittle and hard, but fresh and moist inside. Toast sandwiches should be served while fresh and warm.

*Cold meats* may be advantageously served in a wide variety of ways for light luncheons, aside from sandwiches.

—*The Comfort Food Cookbook*, circa 1925

# Clam-and-Corn Fritters

*Makes about 18
(2-inch) fritters*

*These puffy-crunchy mouthfuls are a combination of two beloved classics: my mom's corn fritters (possibly from an old Joy of Cooking) and New England clam fritters. Top each one with a tiny dollop of curry mayonnaise or Homemade Tartar Sauce on page 163.*

2 (6-ounce) cans minced clams (about ⅔ cup), drained, reserving ¼ cup clam broth

⅔ cup defrosted frozen or canned corn kernels, drained

¼ cup finely chopped cilantro leaves + 2 tablespoons for the sauce

2 tablespoons finely chopped scallion, including green parts + 1 tablespoon for the sauce

1 tablespoon finely chopped roasted red bell pepper (from a jar is fine)

1 large egg, beaten

¼ cup buttermilk or whole milk

½ cup unbleached all-purpose flour

1 ½ teaspoons baking powder

1/2 teaspoon salt

Pinch of cayenne

Canola or vegetable oil, for frying

½ cup mayonnaise

1 ½ teaspoons hot or mild curry paste, according to taste

Tabasco sauce (optional)

Turn your oven on to warm. Line a baking sheet with paper towels.

In a bowl, blend the clams, corn, the 1/4 cup of cilantro leaves, 2 tablespoons of the scallions, and the cayenne. Stir in the egg, reserved clam broth, and buttermilk.

In a separate bowl, combine the flour, baking powder, salt, and cayenne; stir them into the egg-milk mixture just until smooth.

Heat a large cast-iron skillet over medium-high heat until hot but not smoking, 3 1/2 to 4 minutes. Pour in enough oil to measure about 1/8-inch deep. Spoon the mixture by rounded tablespoons into the skillet, flattening slightly with a spatula, and cook until golden brown, about 2 minutes. With a metal spatula, turn the fritters and fry the other side for about the same time; transfer them to the baking sheet in the oven to keep warm. Continue until all the fritters are cooked.

Combine the mayonnaise, curry paste, remaining cilantro, and scallion in a small bowl. If desired, add Tabasco sauce to taste. Serve the fritters on a platter with a tiny dollop of mayonnaise on top of each one.

# Huevos Rancheros

*Serves 4 to 6*

1 tablespoon canola or vegetable oil

4 ounces chorizo, casing removed and cut into ½-inch cubes

1 medium yellow onion, peeled and sliced crosswise

3 large Italian frying peppers, about 6 inches long

8 large eggs

¼ cup whole or low-fat milk

1 ½ cups (6 ounces) shredded medium or sharp Cheddar cheese

1 cup fresh, defrosted frozen or canned corn kernels, drained

⅓ cup chopped cilantro leaves + sprigs to garnish plates

2 pickled jalapeños, seeds and membranes removed, rinsed and chopped

1 teaspoon salt or to taste

Freshly ground black pepper

3 cups homemade or purchased chunky tomato salsa (see note), warmed

1 ripe avocado, peeled and cut into slices, to garnish (optional)

Canned refried beans, heated (optional)

*The combination of Cheddar cheese, corn, chorizo, onions, and pickled jalapeños makes Mexican farmer-style eggs a tasty and colorful brunch option. Roasted frying peppers, cut in half lengthwise and laid flat in the skillet to cover the bottom before the eggs are poured in, help you to easily loft out each portion. Serve with refried beans and garnish with avocado slices. Once baked, the dish can stay for at least a half an hour in a slow oven.*

Preheat your oven to 400°F.

Lay the peppers directly on a gas or electric burner preheated to the hottest setting and roast until the skins are completely charred on all sides, including the ends, turning with tongs. Peppers can also be roasted under a broiler. Transfer them to a paper bag, close the top and let them steam for about 10 minutes to help remove the skin. Using a paring knife or your fingers, scrape off the blackened skin. Cut them in half lengthwise and remove the stem, seeds, and membranes.

Heat a 10-inch cast-iron skillet over medium-high heat until hot but not smoking, 3 1/2 to 4 minutes. Add the oil, chorizo, and onion and sauté until most of the fat is rendered from the chorizo and the onion is lightly browned, 3 to 4 minutes, stirring often. Using a slotted spoon, remove them to a large bowl. Add the peppers in a single layer, skin-side down, covering as much of the bottom as possible

In a large bowl, beat the eggs and milk until blended. Stir in the cheese, corn, cilantro, jalapeños, and salt and black pepper to taste. Scrape the mixture into the skillet and cook for 1 minute over medium-high heat. Adjust the heat down to medium-low and cook for 10 minutes more.

Transfer the skillet to the middle of the oven, turn the heat down to 325°, and bake until a knife inserted into the center comes out almost clean, 22 to 25 minutes. Remove and let stand for a few minutes before cutting into wedges. Spoon on some salsa and serve with a sprig of cilantro, a few avocado slices, and some refried beans, if desired.

*Note:* There are many recipes for fresh and cooked tomato salsa, as well as some terrific prepared products. I often buy chunky tomato salsa and add a pinch of chipotle chile powder for a hint of smoky heat.

{ *Vegetables & Other Sides* }

*This toothsome cornbread made in a 6-inch skillet feeds two or four friends, depending on how hungry they are. Coarsely ground cornmeal, chopped jalapeños, and corn kernels add flavor and texture. I serve it with softened butter bumped up with a touch of honey or maple syrup. It partners well with My Favorite Chili (page 142), Oven-Roasted Chicken (page 88), or Caesar salads.*

*A well-seasoned cast-iron skillet is essential for the crisp edges and golden brown crust. To preserve the crunchy texture, turn the bread onto a plate while still hot and leave it bottom-side up or serve it directly from the pan. This recipe is easily doubled. You'll also find those small skillets have a lot of other uses. (See note.)*

# Mini Cast-Iron Skillet Cornbread

## Serves 2 to 4

Preheat your oven to 450°F. Put a 6-inch cast-iron skillet in the oven for 15 minutes to heat. Meanwhile combine the cornmeal, flour, sugar, baking powder, and salt in a bowl. Stir in the corn and jalapeños. In a separate bowl, whisk together the buttermilk, 4 tablespoons of the butter, and the egg; stir the wet mixture into the dry ingredients until just blended.

Remove the skillet from the oven, brush with the remaining tablespoon of butter, and spoon in the batter, smoothing the top with a metal spatula. Bake until the top of the cornbread is golden and a toothpick inserted in the center comes out clean, 23 to 25 minutes. Remove, and let stand on a rack for

¾ cup coarsely ground yellow cornmeal

¼ cup unbleached all-purpose flour

1 tablespoon sugar

1 teaspoon baking powder

½ teaspoon salt

½ cup defrosted frozen or canned corn kernels, drained

2 tablespoons chopped pickled jalapeño peppers

½ cup buttermilk

5 tablespoons melted unsalted butter

1 large egg

a few minutes before inverting (or serve the cornbread out of the pan). Serve with softened butter.

*Note:* Mini cast-iron skillets make appealing individual serving containers. For example, the Chocolate Chunk-Pecan Cookie Sundaes with Salted Caramel Sauce (page 200) are a decadent way to finish your dinner. Or, as Elyse Harney (whose husband's duck recipe is on page 110) suggests, they are the perfect answer to breakfast for the "me generation." Elyse puts a small skillet on each of her stove's six burners and lets everyone make his or her eggs to their own taste. Some like them up; others prefer them over or scrambled, she says.

# *Aunt Ellen's* Delicious Kitchen Tested Dishes

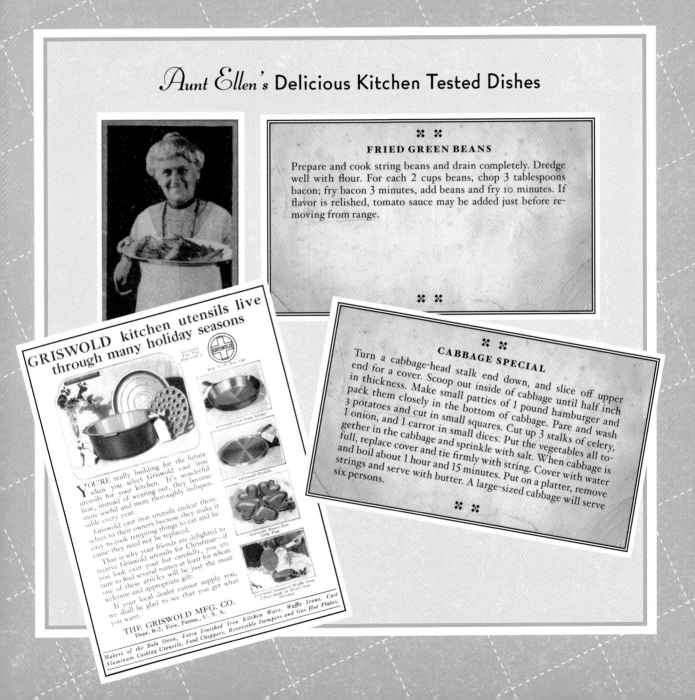

### ❈ ❈
### FRIED GREEN BEANS

Prepare and cook string beans and drain completely. Dredge well with flour. For each 2 cups beans, chop 3 tablespoons bacon; fry bacon 3 minutes, add beans and fry 10 minutes. If flavor is relished, tomato sauce may be added just before removing from range.

### ❈ ❈

### ❈ ❈
### CABBAGE SPECIAL

Turn a cabbage-head stalk end down, and slice off upper end for a cover. Scoop out inside of cabbage until half inch in thickness. Make small patties of 1 pound hamburger and pack them closely in the bottom of cabbage. Pare and wash 3 potatoes and cut in small squares. Cut up 3 stalks of celery, 1 onion, and 1 carrot in small dices. Put the vegetables all together in the cabbage and sprinkle with salt. When cabbage is full, replace cover and tie firmly with string. Cover with water and boil about 1 hour and 15 minutes. Put on a platter, remove strings and serve with butter. A large-sized cabbage will serve six persons.

### ❈ ❈

# Sweet and Tangy Glazed Carrots with Cranberries

*Serves 4*

*When honey and vinegar plus a handful of dried cranberries are reduced to glaze young carrots, it becomes a memorable side dish to enjoy for holidays or anytime you want a special vegetable. I like thyme honey because it adds a slightly bitter taste to the complex flavors, but any variety works. These can be made ahead and reheated.*

1 ½ pounds young carrots, peeled or large carrots cut lengthwise into quarters and in half widthwise

1 tablespoon canola or vegetable oil

1 teaspoon salt

½ cup good-quality chicken stock

1 tablespoon unsalted butter

¼ cup dried cranberries

2 tablespoons thyme honey or other variety

2 tablespoons sherry or white wine vinegar

1 tablespoon finely chopped flat-leaf parsley

Combine the carrots, oil, and salt in a bowl. Heat a cast-iron skillet large enough to hold the carrots in a single layer over medium heat until just hot, about 3 1/2 minutes. Scrape the carrots into the pan oil and cook for 2 minutes, stirring once or twice. Stir in the stock and butter, cover the skillet, reduce the heat to low, and cook for 15 minutes or until the carrots are almost tender when pierced with the tip of a knife.

Remove the lid and stir in the cranberries, honey, and vinegar. Bring to a boil and cook until the liquid reduces to glaze the carrots, about 5 minutes, shaking the pan occasionally. Stir in the parsley and serve.

# Glazed Butternut Squash

*Serves 4 to 6*

*Butternut squash, luxuriously glazed with brown sugar, maple syrup, and bourbon, is so delicious, you may find everyone asking for seconds. The touch of minced fresh rosemary adds an exciting counterpoint to the sweet flavors. A few months ago I went looking for butternut squash and discovered that it is now more often sold already peeled and cubed, a welcome convenience. This colorful side dish dresses up holiday turkeys, Oven-Roasted Chicken, or Pan-Seared Pork Chops (page 150).*

1 ¼ pounds peeled butternut squash, cut into 1-inch chunks

1 tablespoon canola or vegetable oil

Salt and freshly ground black pepper

2 tablespoons unsalted butter

2 tablespoons firmly packed dark brown sugar

2 tablespoons light amber maple syrup

2 tablespoons bourbon

2 teaspoons minced fresh rosemary leaves (optional)

Toss the squash with the oil, about 1 teaspoon of salt, and pepper to taste. Heat a 10-inch cast-iron skillet over medium-high heat until hot but not smoking, 3 1/2 to 4 minutes. Add the squash and cook until lightly browned on all sides, about 5 minutes, turning often.

Add the butter, brown sugar, and maple syrup; bring to a boil, and cook until the sugar is melted, turning to coat the squash. Off the heat, carefully pour in the bourbon (it might flame) and cook until the flames subside. Cover and cook over medium heat until the squash is almost tender, about 10 minutes, then uncover and gently reduce the liquid until it glazes the squash, about 3 minutes more, turning often. Stir in the rosemary, if using, and serve.

*Whether you call them* latkes *or* röstis—*a Swiss specialty—or just potato pancakes, shredded and fried potatoes have many fans. Here I use sweet potatoes or yams (I prefer the latter), hazelnuts, and shallots for a scrumptious side dish. Unlike the Zucchini Pancakes on page 66, these should be cooked soon after the ingredients are mixed.*

# Sweet Potato Röstis

*Serves 4*

Preheat your oven to 400°F.

In a large bowl, cover the shredded sweet potato with warm water. Sprinkle with about 1/2 tablespoon of salt and let them stand for 5 minutes; drain and squeeze the potatoes very dry in a clean towel or with your hands. Wipe out the bowl and return the potatoes along with the shallots, hazelnuts, parsley, egg, salt, and pepper, and mix well. Divide the rösti mixture into 4 equal portions.

Heat a 12- or 13-inch cast-iron skillet over medium-high heat until hot but not smoking, 3 1/2 to 4 minutes. Add 2 tablespoons of the oil and the rösti portions to the pan all at the same time, gently flattening them with a spatula into 3 1/2-inch discs. Drizzle the remaining oil over the röstis, then transfer the skillet to the oven and bake until they are nicely browned and crunchy on the bottom, about 30 minutes. Carefully turn them over and return the pan to the oven for 10 minutes. Serve garnished with a little parsley.

1 pound yams or sweet potatoes, peeled and coarsely shredded

Coarse or kosher salt

½ cup finely chopped shallots

⅓ cup hazelnuts, roasted and coarsely chopped (see note below)

2 tablespoons finely chopped flat-leaf parsley + extra for garnish

1 large egg, beaten

½ teaspoon salt or to taste

Freshly ground black pepper

3 tablespoons olive oil

*Note*: Spread the whole nuts in a single layer on a baking sheet and bake at 275°F for 20 to 30 minutes until lightly browned. While still warm, transfer them to a slightly damp towel and rub briskly to remove the skins.

*Many vegetables other than potatoes can be shredded and fried into tasty pancakes. I particularly like this combination of zucchini, scallions, dill, oregano, feta, and pine nuts. It reminds me of a pancake-like hors d'oeuvre called mücver that I've eaten on several occasions in Turkey. Serve the pancakes with a dab of Red Pepper–Yogurt Sauce or simply, as Turks do, with plain yogurt on top, either as a side dish or a nibble before a meal.*

# Zucchini Pancakes
## *Serves 6*

In a colander, toss the zucchini with about 1/2 tablespoon of salt and drain for 20 to 25 minutes. Meanwhile, prepare the Red Pepper–Yogurt Sauce, if using, and set aside.

Working in batches, squeeze the zucchini with your hands to remove as much moisture as possible, then transfer it to a kitchen towel or several layers of paper towels and squeeze again. In a bowl, combine the zucchini, eggs, scallions, dill, mint or parsley, about 1/2 teaspoon of salt, and a generous amount of pepper, and mix well. Stir in the flour, then add the feta, and stir to blend. Just before cooking, stir in the pine nuts.

Preheat your oven to 300°F. Line a baking sheet with paper towels and put it in the oven.

Heat a 12-inch cast-iron skillet or griddle over medium-high heat. Add enough oil to coat the bottom of the pan. Drop the zucchini mixture by generous soup-spoonfuls into the skillet

1 pound zucchini, trimmed and coarsely grated by hand or in a food processor

Coarse or kosher salt

2 large eggs, beaten

1 cup chopped scallions, including most of the green parts

⅓ cup chopped fresh dill or 1 ½ tablespoons dried dillweed

⅓ cup chopped fresh mint or flat-leaf parsley

Freshly ground black pepper

½ cup unbleached all-purpose flour

½ cup crumbled feta cheese

½ cup pine nuts

Olive oil, for frying

Red Pepper-Yogurt Sauce (recipe follows)

(about 3 tablespoons) and flatten with the back of a spatula into 3-inch discs, cooking only as many pancakes as will fit comfortably without crowding. Fry until golden brown, 2 1/2 to 3 minutes, then turn and fry the other side for the same length of time. Transfer the pancakes to the baking sheet to keep warm while frying the remaining pancakes. Serve hot.

## Red Pepper–Yogurt Sauce

1 large roasted red bell pepper (from a jar is fine), blotted dry

1 clove garlic, peeled

¼ teaspoon salt

2 tablespoons Greek-style (thick) plain yogurt

1 tablespoon extra-virgin olive oil

2 tablespoons chopped fresh mint leaves

In the jar of an electric blender or food processor, purée the bell pepper, garlic, and salt until smooth. Scrape into a small bowl and stir in the olive oil. Add the mint just before serving.

# Brussels Sprouts with Bacon and Pistachios

*Serves 4*

*Forget the old-fashioned notion that everyone hates Brussels sprouts. This version—or one similar to it—is served by many of today's best restaurants to great acclaim. The Brussels sprouts are blanched in salted water to keep them bright green, then finished with bacon and pistachios. I use relatively lean bacon from my favorite butcher Sal Biancardi on Arthur Avenue, in the Bronx.*

1 pound Brussels sprouts, outer leaves removed, cored and quartered lengthwise

Kosher salt

3 slices thick-cut bacon, diced (about 4 ounces)

Leaves from 2 sprigs fresh thyme, chopped

¼ cup (2 ounces) shelled pistachios

Freshly ground black pepper

Bring a pot of salted water to a boil. Add the Brussels sprouts and cook until just tender, about 3 minutes. Drain, rinse under very cold water to stop the cooking, and blot dry on a clean towel.

Meanwhile, put the bacon into a large cast-iron skillet and cook over medium heat until most of the fat is rendered, 3 to 4 minutes, stirring often. Add the thyme, Brussels sprouts, and pistachios and cook until heated through, turning often. Season to taste with salt and pepper, and serve.

72

*Wild mushrooms are so versatile and plentiful, especially during fall and winter months. I serve this robust mixture as a side dish or on top of Pan-Seared Pork Chops (page 150), as well as with chicken or swordfish.*

# Oven-Roasted Wild Mushrooms
## *Serves 4*

Preheat your oven to 400°F. Chop the garlic, oregano, and salt together until minced.

Heat a 10-inch cast-iron skillet over medium-high heat until hot but not smoking, 3 1/2 to 4 minutes. Add 1 tablespoon of the oil and the onion and sauté until lightly browned, about 3 minutes, stirring them occasionally. Add the remaining oil, the mushrooms, garlic-oregano mixture, red pepper flakes, and a liberal amount of black pepper. Cook for 1 minute, turning to coat the mushrooms with the seasonings and oil.

Transfer the skillet to the oven and cook until the mushrooms are golden brown and limp, about 12 minutes, stirring once or twice. Remove to the stovetop and, over high heat, stir in the balsamic vinegar. Cook for 1 minute to reduce the vinegar; taste to adjust the seasonings, sprinkle on the parsley, and serve.

3 large cloves garlic, peeled

3 tablespoons chopped fresh oregano leaves

2 teaspoons salt

3 tablespoons olive oil

1 large yellow onion, peeled and thinly sliced

1 pound mixed wild mushrooms, such as porcini, shiitake, and oyster mushrooms, wiped, trimmed, and sliced

Pinch of red pepper flakes

Freshly ground black pepper

1 tablespoon high-quality balsamic vinegar

1 tablespoon chopped flat-leaf parsley, to garnish

# Oven-Roasted Asparagus with Macadamia Nuts

## Serves 4

1 pound medium asparagus, woody ends snapped off

1 tablespoon extra-virgin olive oil

Coarse sea or kosher salt and freshly ground black pepper

1 tablespoon unsalted butter

2 tablespoons chopped macadamia nuts

1 teaspoon grated lemon zest

*If you haven't tasted asparagus roasted in the oven in a cast-iron skillet, you're in for a treat. The beautiful green stalks gain a depth of flavor impossible to achieve by simply boiling or steaming. Topped with chopped macadamia nuts and a little lemon zest, they are irresistible.*

Preheat your oven to 450°F.

Heat a 10-inch cast-iron skillet over medium-high heat until hot but not smoking, 3 1/2 to 4 minutes. Add the asparagus, oil, about 1/2 teaspoon salt, and black pepper to taste, and shake to coat evenly. Place the skillet in the oven and roast until the stalks are bright green and crisp-tender with little char spots, about 10 minutes (or longer if you prefer them softer), shaking the pan occasionally.

Meanwhile, melt the butter in a small skillet over medium heat. Add the macadamias and cook until lightly browned, 2 to 3 minutes, watching that they don't burn. Stir in the lemon zest and keep warm over low heat.

When the asparagus are cooked, pour on the macadamia nuts and butter, turning to coat the stalks evenly, and serve.

"We may dine in two or three languages as Irvin Cobb says, and get thin and willowy, (on chicken and croquettes and Mexican Chili), but a wise and solemn gentlemen rises to remark that the world is going to the dogs, (on canapes and spaghetti) and that something ought to be done to bring back the delectable cooking of our mothers and grandmothers."

-Aunt Ellen

*In this elegant side dish, oven-roasted fennel's mild anise flavor is topped with nutty-tasting Gruyère and bread crumbs. The optional light cream adds a touch of richness. You can cook this ahead and gently reheat it.*

# Fennel Gratin
## *Serves 4*

Preheat your oven to 375°F. Finely chop together the garlic, 1/2 tablespoon of the rosemary leaves, and the salt.

Heat a very large cast-iron skillet over medium-high heat until hot but not smoking, 3 1/2 to 4 minutes, and lightly brush with oil. Lay the fennel slices in the skillet in a single layer; sprinkle on the rosemary mixture, and season liberally with black pepper.

In a small bowl, combine the Gruyère, panko, and remaining rosemary leaves; sprinkle them evenly over the fennel, drizzle on the remaining olive oil, and bake until tender when pierced with a knife and the top is bubbling and nicely browned, 40 to 50 minutes. If using the cream, drizzle it on after about 20 minutes, and continue baking, as above.

1 large clove garlic, peeled

1 ½ tablespoons chopped fresh rosemary leaves, divided

1 teaspoon salt

2 tablespoons extra-virgin olive oil

2 fennel bulbs, trimmed, cored, and cut crosswise into ³/₈-inch slices

Freshly ground black pepper

¹/₃ cup grated Gruyère, Comté, or other Swiss cheese

¹/₃ cup panko bread crumbs, found in the Asian food section of supermarkets

¹/₄ cup light cream (optional)

# Cheesy Stone-Ground Grits

*Serves 6*

*If you haven't tried slowly simmered grits, liberally laced with Cheddar cheese, you're in for a treat. Although instant and quick-cooking grits are easier to find, coarse-ground grits produce an incomparably toothy yet creamy texture and satisfying taste. Given a choice, white grits are preferable to yellow because they are less starchy, but both are delicious. Grits are great with the simplest chicken or fish dish, and they make a decadent partner for All-American Short Ribs (page 132).*

*Like hominy (see page 180), grits are a Native American corn product. The dried and processed corn kernels are coarsely ground on a stone mill. In the South, devotees enjoy them at every meal from breakfast straight through dinner and dessert. I've found cooking times for grits from different suppliers can vary from under an hour to 2 hours. Stir the pot frequently, especially the bottom, with a flexible scraper and wait until after you've added the cheese to add salt.*

2+ cups chicken stock

2 cups whole milk

1 cup coarse stone-ground grits, preferably white

1 tablespoon unsalted butter

2 cups (8 ounce) shredded sharp white Cheddar cheese

Salt

Tabasco or other hot sauce (optional)

Combine 2 cups of stock and the milk in a 10-inch cast-iron Dutch oven and bring a boil. Add the grits, stirring continuously until blended and smooth. Turn the heat down to low and simmer according to the package directions until the grits are tender, about 1 hour (some brands can take up to 2 hours), stirring frequently with a flexible scraper to prevent the grits from sticking to the bottom of the pan.

If the mixture gets thick and starts to dry out, stir in more liquid—water or stock by 1/4-cupfuls—until smooth. Once the grits are done, stir in the butter and cheese and cook until melted. Season to taste with salt and Tabasco sauce, if desired, before serving.

*If you're a fan of baked beans with a little heat, this simple version—emboldened with chipotle chiles in adobo sauce—will assuredly excite your taste buds. Double-smoked bacon helps reinforce the barbecue flavors.*

# Blazin' Baked Beans
## Serves 12

Put the beans in a large cast-iron Dutch oven with enough water to cover. Bring to a boil and cook for 3 minutes; turn off the heat, cover, and let them stand for 1 hour. Drain, cover again with water, add salt, and bring to a boil for 5 minutes, then reduce the heat to a simmer, cover, and cook for 30 minutes more. Remove from the heat, pour the beans and their liquid into a large bowl, and let them stand in the liquid until cooled.

Meanwhile, preheat your oven to 250°F.

Sauté the bacon in the Dutch oven over medium heat until it is crisp, turning often. Remove, blot on paper towels, and set aside. Reserve 2 tablespoons of fat in the pot, or add enough oil to make 2 tablespoons, and heat over medium-high heat. Add the onions and sauté until golden brown, 3 to 4 minutes.

Drain the beans and combine them with the bacon, onions, chipotle chiles, mustard, brown sugar, and barbecue sauce. Add enough boiling water to just cover the beans, cover the pot, and bake for 4 hours. Remove the lid for the last 30 minutes of cooking time, or until the liquid is reduced and the beans are very tender. Taste to adjust the seasonings, adding salt if needed. Let them stand for 15 minutes before serving.

2 pounds pea or navy beans, rinsed and picked over

1 tablespoon salt or to taste

1/2 pound thick sliced bacon, finely diced

2 tablespoons bacon fat or vegetable oil

1 1/2 cups chopped yellow onions

2 chipotle chiles in adobo sauce, finely chopped

1/3 cup Dijon mustard

1/3 cup firmly packed dark brown sugar

1 (18-ounce) jar high-quality smoky barbecue sauce

Boiling water

# Block Party Baked Beans

*Serves about 18*

*If you don't have time to make Blazin' Baked Beans (page 80), Sarah Collins comes to the rescue with her "speed scratch" recipe for block parties, picnics, barbecues, and other outdoor events when a variety of easy foods are offered. This recipe can simmer in the oven while you help set up tables and keep score for the kids' badminton games. It pairs well with anything else that's on the picnic table. Your serving pot will be empty at the end of the party!*

6 slices bacon, cut into 1-inch pieces

3 (28-ounce) cans Campbell's Pork & Beans

1 tablespoons Dijon mustard

¼ cup tomato ketchup

3 tablespoons firmly packed dark brown sugar

Preheat your oven to 300° or 325°F.

Put the bacon in a large cast-iron Dutch oven and cook over medium heat until the bacon is crisp and has rendered its fat, 4 to 5 minutes, stirring often. Drain the fat and add the baked beans (with their liquid), mustard, ketchup, and brown sugar. Cover and simmer in the oven for 1 to 2 hours, stirring occasionally. Serve in the Dutch oven.

{ *Main Courses* }

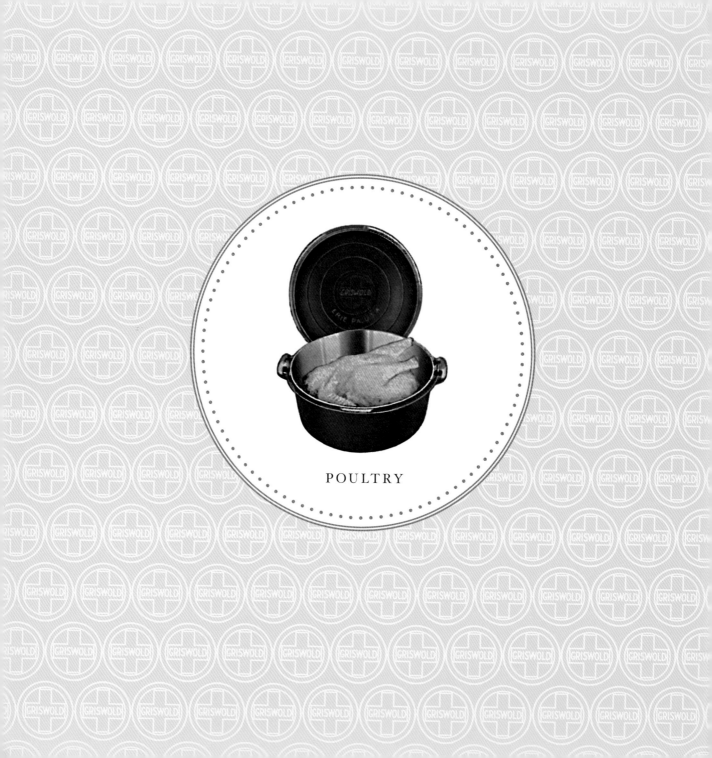

POULTRY

"The seductive smells from such a kitchen sent a summons sharp as bells . . . Portly smells—from guinea hens soaked in wine juice. . . . birds broiling over ashes . . . white onions stewing in a ruddy pan. They made life genial for the eating."

-Aunt Ellen

*I love crisp, juicy, oven-roasted chicken and, once you taste it cooked this way, I think you'll be won over, too. Here, I offer two ways to prepare and serve it: au natural—simply cooked in the hot pan without any fuss—or with chopped vegetables roasted in the same pan that can then be served alongside the chicken or puréed with a little white wine and stock into delicious pan gravy. While the chicken's bottom may be slightly less crisp when cooked with the vegetables, the trade-off is a delicious addition to your meal.*

*If you have time, put the uncovered chicken in the refrigerator the night before to let the skin tighten and help seal in the flavor and moisture.*

Rinse the chicken inside and out under cold water and pat very dry with paper towels. Season the cavity with salt and pepper, add the rosemary and thyme, and squeeze in the lemon juice. Put the lemon half inside the cavity, and refrigerate the chicken on a cake rack over a plate overnight, or for at least 8 hours.

Preheat your oven to 450°F. While the oven heats, remove the chicken from the refrigerator and let it return to room temperature; tie the legs together with string, turn the wingtips under, and pat the chicken dry again.

Melt the butter in a 10-inch cast-iron skillet over medium-high heat or heat the oil until hot and brush it on the chicken.

# Oven-Roasted Chicken with Pan Gravy
## *Serves 4*

1 (3 ½-pound) frying chicken, with neck, giblets, and extra fat removed

Kosher or coarse salt and freshly ground black pepper

2 sprigs fresh rosemary

2 sprigs fresh thyme

½ lemon

2 tablespoons unsalted butter or olive oil

1 large yellow onion, peeled, cut in half crosswise and quartered

1 large stalk celery, trimmed and coarsely chopped

1 medium carrot, peeled and coarsely chopped

¼ cup dry white wine, such as sauvignon blanc

½ cup chicken stock, heated

2 tablespoons chopped flat-leaf parsley

Lay the chicken breast-side up in the pan, transfer it to the oven with the legs facing toward the back and roast for 10 minutes. If using the vegetables, scatter them around but not under the chicken, baste with the pan juices, and sprinkle on a generous amount of salt. Continue roasting until the skin is a rich golden brown, turning the vegetables a couple of times. Begin testing the chicken for doneness after 55 minutes. If the juices run clear when the flesh is pricked deep in the thigh joint, it is done.

Transfer the chicken to a heated platter to rest for 10 to 15 minutes while finishing the gravy, if serving.

For the pan gravy: Put the skillet over high heat, pour in the wine, and bring to a boil, stirring up the browned cooking bits; cook 2 to 3 minutes, then scrape the pan drippings into the jar of an electric blender and purée until smooth. Add the chicken stock, taste to adjust the seasonings, and return the gravy to the skillet to keep warm. Stir in the parsley.

Cut the chicken into pieces and serve with a generous spoonful of pan gravy. Pass the remaining gravy at the table. Alternatively, spoon off as much fat as possible from the skillet and serve the roasted vegetables and pan juices with the chicken.

# Italian Brick-Roasted Chicken *(Pollo al Mattone)*

*Serves 4*

For centuries, Italians have pan roasted crispy, juicy chickens using a foil-wrapped brick, or mattone, as a weight on top of the bird to keep it flat and ensure even cooking. When cayenne or red pepper flakes are in the marinade, it is known as chicken alla diavolo, or devil's fare, because of the bird's charred flesh and peppery taste.

If you don't want to remove the breastbone, as suggested below, you can buy a split chicken. Dry the skin well to prevent the skin from sticking or tearing when turning the bird over. A second cast-iron skillet works well as a weight on top of the chicken so long as it does not completely cover the first pan (which would cause it to steam). Serve the chicken hot or at room temperature with roasted potatoes.

1 (3-pound) frying chicken, rinsed and patted dry

2 sprigs rosemary

3 sprigs fresh thyme

2 large cloves garlic, peeled

Coarse sea salt

1/2 cup olive oil

1/3 cup fresh lemon juice + 1 lemon, cut into wedges, for garnish

1 teaspoon Tabasco sauce (optional)

1 brick, wrapped in heavy aluminum foil, or a second cast-iron skillet

Cut off the first 2 wing joints from the chickens and discard. Trim off any excess skin and fat. Remove the backbone by cutting along either side of the spine with kitchen shears. Open the bird flat, turning the bird flesh-side down with the legs closest to you. Starting at the bottom point of the breastbone, run the tip of a knife along the bone, pulling up on the cartilage and bone to work it loose from the breasts, taking care not to tear the skin. Flip the rib cage back and chop off the bones. Make an incision between the skin of the leg and thigh, partially separating the two sections. Repeat with the breast and wing sections.

Remove the leaves from the rosemary and thyme sprigs; finely chop them with the garlic and 1 tablespoon of salt. Rub the mixture over the chicken and put it in a large, resealable plastic bag. Pour in the oil, lemon juice, and Tabasco sauce. Seal the bag and marinate in the refrigerator for at least 4 hours or overnight, turning once or twice.

About an hour before cooking, remove the chicken from the refrigerator to return to room temperature. Remove it from the marinade and dry very well with paper towels.

Heat a 10-inch cast-iron skillet over high heat until very hot and almost smoking, about 4 minutes. Brush it with oil, lay the chicken skin-side down in the pan, and immediately place the foil-covered brick or second pan on top, pressing down to flatten it. Let the chicken cook undisturbed until the skin is browned and crisp, about 12 minutes. Remove the brick, turn the bird over, replace the brick, and cook the other side for 10 minutes, or until the juices run clear when the chicken is pricked in the deepest part of the thigh.

Transfer the chicken to a warm platter, tent with aluminum foil, and let it stand for 15 minutes before cutting it into leg and breast portions, then serve garnished with lemon wedges.

# Chicken Paprikás

*Serves 4*

*For many Magyárs (Hungarians), including some of my great-grandparents, braised chicken lavishly seasoned with paprika and enriched with sour cream was comfort food. It's still satisfying today. Although I use less sour cream than those heartier folks, feel free to indulge and add more than what I suggest, if you'd like. There is plenty of sauce in this dish to serve over boiled noodles or dumplings. This is a great meal to make ahead and gently reheat (do not boil) before serving.*

1 (3 ½-pound) frying chicken, excess fat and skin trimmed

Unbleached all-purpose flour for dredging + 1 tablespoons flour for sauce

Salt and freshly ground black pepper

2 tablespoons canola or vegetable oil

1 large yellow onion, peeled and finely chopped

½ cup chicken stock or water

2 tablespoons Hungarian paprika, sweet or hot or a combination (see note)

3+ tablespoons regular or reduced-fat sour cream

½ tablespoon tomato paste

1 green bell pepper, seeds and membranes removed, and diced

4 ounces white mushrooms, trimmed, wiped and sliced

Chopped flat-leaf parsley, to garnish

Rinse the chicken under water and pat dry with paper towels. Remove and discard the wings. Cut the chicken into 8 serving pieces, cutting the breasts in half. Dredge the chicken pieces in flour, patting to remove any excess; generously season them with salt and pepper.

Heat a 10-inch cast-iron Dutch oven over medium-high heat until hot but not smoking, 3 1/2 to 4 minutes. Add the oil and chicken, skin-side down, and cook until browned, about 5 minutes. Turn the pieces and brown the other side, then remove them to a bowl.

Stir in the onions and cook until limp, 2 to 3 minutes. Add the stock and paprika, and cook 1 minute longer. Return the chicken to the pot, cover, reduce the heat, and simmer for about 25 minutes, stirring occasionally. Remove the chicken to a bowl.

In a small bowl, combine the remaining tablespoon of flour with 1 tablespoon of cold water, the sour cream, and tomato paste; stir it into the pot until smooth. Add the bell pepper and mushrooms along with the chicken. Cover and simmer until the chicken is cooked through and the vegetables are tender, about 10 minutes. Taste to adjust the seasonings, and serve over noodles or dumplings sprinkled with a little parsley.

*Note:* Hungarian paprika is sold in both hot and sweet varieties. To preserve the flavor and pungency of paprika, buy it in small quantities and store in an airtight container in a cool, dark spot.

# Old-Fashioned Buttermilk Fried Chicken

*Serves 4*

*More than fifty years ago, when my friend Stephen Kahan was growing up in Virginia, he loved the crunchy fried chicken that his family's housekeeper made. She removed the skin, cut the chicken into small pieces, and soaked it overnight in buttermilk before coating it with seasoned flour followed by crushed cornflakes and grated cheese. The pieces were browned on top of the stove in a little oil and finished in the oven. I added Mom's Seasoning Mix (page 103) to the flour and some herbs to the buttermilk. (Similar recipes appeared on cereal boxes at least fifty years ago; see sidebar on next page.)*

1 (3- to 3 ¼-pound) frying chicken, skin and extra fat removed

2 cups buttermilk

2 tablespoons Tabasco or other hot sauce

2 teaspoons salt

1 teaspoon each dried tarragon, thyme, and garlic powder

1 ½ cups unbleached all-purpose flour

Salt and freshly ground black pepper or 1 ½ tablespoons Mom's Seasoning Mix (see page 103)

4 cups cornflakes, finely crushed (about 1 cup crushed crumbs)

1 cup grated Parmesan cheese

Peanut, grapeseed, or canola oil, for frying

Remove and discard the wings, if desired. Cut the breast into two or three pieces and, if the thighs are large, cut them in half. Combine the chicken, buttermilk, Tabasco sauce, tarragon, thyme, and garlic powder in a 1-gallon resealable plastic bag, turning to coat all sides; seal and refrigerate for at least 8 hours or overnight.

Preheat your oven to 450°F. Spray a wire rack with nonstick vegetable spray and put it on a baking sheet covered with aluminum foil in the oven. Heat a 12-inch cast-iron skillet over medium-high heat until hot but not smoking, 3 1/2 to 4 minutes.

Meanwhile, drain the chicken in a strainer or colander and discard the buttermilk. Combine the flour with the salt and pepper (or Mom's Seasoning Mix) in a large bowl. In another bowl, combine the cornflakes and cheese. Pour enough oil into the skillet to cover the bottom by 1/8 to 1/4 inch.

Dip the chicken in the flour mixture, patting to remove the excess. Roll the chicken pieces in the crumbs, pressing firmly to coat thoroughly, and put them in the pan, allowing a little time for the fat to reheat with each addition. Add the dark meat first, and only as many pieces as will fit comfortably without crowding. Fry until light golden brown on both sides, turning once, 4 to 5 minutes per side. Using metal tongs, transfer the chicken to the oven and bake until cooked through, 20 to 25 minutes, or when it an instant-read thermometer reads about 170°F when inserted in the thickest part of the meat next to the bone.

# Southern Fried Chicken

*Serves 4*

*For die-hard, "real" fried chicken lovers who believe the best reason to own a cast-iron skillet is to fry chicken in it, you are correct: the pan's weight retains and distributes the heat evenly as the pieces of chicken are added to the fat so they develop that crunchy crust we aspire to. It's essential that the fat continues to sizzle but doesn't get too hot, which would burn the outside before the meat is done. The chicken is done when it an instant-read thermometer reads about 170°F when inserted in the thickest part of the meat next to the bone. The soaking and coating seasonings are my suggestions; use whatever pleases your palate.*

1 (3- to 3 ¼-pound) frying chicken, extra fat removed, cut into serving pieces

2 cups buttermilk

2 tablespoons Tabasco or other hot sauce

2 teaspoons salt

2 teaspoons each dried tarragon, thyme, and garlic powder

2 cups unbleached all-purpose flour

2 tablespoons Southern Seasoning Mix (page 151) or 1 tablespoon each paprika, salt, and ground pepper + ⅛ teaspoon cayenne

Crisco or other solid vegetable shortening, or vegetable oil, for frying

In a large, resealable plastic bag, combine the chicken, buttermilk, Tabasco, salt, garlic powder, tarragon, and thyme; seal the bag, turn several times to coat evenly, and refrigerate overnight or for at least 8 hours, turning the bag a couple of times.

If you are cooking the chicken in batches, or more than one chicken, turn your oven to warm. Put a wire rack coated with nonstick vegetable spray over a baking sheet covered with aluminum foil in the oven

Combine the flour and Southern Seasoning Mix or seasonings in a plastic or brown paper bag. Remove the chicken from the buttermilk mixture and drain in a colander or strainer. It shouldn't be totally dry.

In a large 12-inch cast-iron skillet, melt enough shortening over medium heat to measure about 1/2 inch deep and heat until hot; or heat the skillet until just hot, about 3 minutes, and pour in the oil. When a little flour sprinkled on the oil foams, the fat is hot enough. It shouldn't be smoking. If it is, turn off the heat and let it cool a little.

Toss the chicken pieces in the seasoned flour, patting to remove the excess. Gradually add them to the fat, taking care not to crowd the pan, and always allowing time for the fat to come back up to heat. Add the dark pieces first. Cook until golden brown, about 10 minutes; turn and cook the other side until golden, 8 to 10 minutes. Transfer the chicken pieces to the rack in the oven to keep warm if you do this in batches. Or, blot on paper towels. Serve with corn on the cob or Mini Cast-Iron Skillet Cornbread and a mixed green salad, if desired.

# Mom's Chicken in a Pot

*Serves 4*

*The smell of this chicken as it cooks, more than any other food, reminds me of my mom's kitchen. The seasonings—especially Lawry's Seasoning Salt, created in 1938 for their Prime Rib restaurant in Beverly Hills—are very much of her era. When I found a deconstructed version of the salt on the Web, I was delighted because I'm allergic to the MSG in the original. I combined it with the other seasonings my mom used for this homey, delicious chicken.*

1 (3- to 3 ½-pound) frying chicken, excess fat and skinned removed

2 teaspoons canola or vegetable oil

1 medium yellow onion, peeled and sliced

1 to 1 ½ tablespoons Mom's Seasoning Mix

2 canned tomatoes, drained and chopped

Rinse the chicken under cold water and pat dry with paper towels. Preheat your oven to 325°F.

Heat a 10-inch cast-iron Dutch oven over medium-high heat until hot but not smoking, 3 1/2 to 4 minutes. Add the oil and onion, and cook until lightly browned, 3 to 4 minutes.

Meanwhile, season the chicken inside and out with the seasoning mix. Tie the legs together. Lay the whole chicken on its back on top of the onion, add the tomatoes, cover, and cook for 45 minutes, basting occasionally. Prick the flesh deep in the thigh joint to see if the juices run almost clear.

Uncover the pot and turn on your broiler. Turn the chicken to one side to brown the skin, about 3 minutes, watching that it doesn't burn. Turn, baste, and brown the other side; finally turn it on its back to brown the breast. Remove the chicken from the pot, cut it into quarters, and serve over boiled noodles or rice. Pass extra gravy at the table.

# Mom's Seasoning Mix

1 $\frac{1}{2}$ tablespoons salt

1 tablespoon sweet paprika

1 teaspoon celery salt

$\frac{1}{4}$ teaspoon each freshly ground black pepper, turmeric, onion powder, garlic powder, and cornstarch

In a small bowl, combine the ingredients and mix well; store in a small bottle.

# Roast Turkey Breast London Broil

*Serves 4*

My friend Sally Kofke introduced me to this remarkable high-heat method for cooking turkey London broil—half of a boneless, skinless turkey breast—in a cast-iron skillet. It's easy, with results that are incredibly succulent. Sally likes Renaissance Rub—a mixture of rosemary, sesame seed, red pepper, oregano, minced garlic, dried tomato, and lemon peel—but anything from Jamaican Jerk seasoning to my Southern Seasoning Mix (page 151) will work well. Ready-made rubs often cost less than purchasing the ingredients and mixing them at home.

1 (2-pound) turkey London broil

Coarse or kosher salt

Freshly ground black pepper

Olive oil

1 tablespoon purchased or homemade seasoning rub (see recipe notes)

2/3 cup dry white wine

1 cup low-sodium chicken stock

2 tablespoons Dijon mustard

1/2 cup heavy cream

Few drops fresh lemon juice

1 tablespoon finely chopped tarragon or herb of your choice according to the flavors of the rub

Preheat your oven to 500°F.

Turn the turkey, flesh-side up, and pat dry; using a sharp knife, lightly score through the membrane in a 1-inch diagonal pattern. Season with about 3/4 teaspoon salt and 1/2 teaspoon pepper, pressing them firmly into the flesh with the palm of your hand. Turn the breast over onto a sheet of waxed paper and dry the other side; brush with olive oil and sprinkle with the rub, patting it in place.

Heat a cast-iron skillet without any oil until smoking. Carefully place the turkey, salt-and-peppered side down, into the pan. Sear the turkey until it no longer sticks to the pan, 2 to 3 minutes. Do not turn. Immediately transfer the skillet to the lower third of the oven and cook for 15 to 20 minutes or until the temperature reads 160° on an instant-read meat thermometer. Remove, transfer the turkey to a warm platter, and loosely tent with foil.

On top of the stove over high heat, deglaze the skillet with the white wine and reduce to about 1/4 cup. Add the chicken stock and reduce by half; whisk in the mustard, then the heavy cream, and bring to a boil; reduce the heat and simmer until thickened. Season to taste with salt, pepper, and lemon juice, and stir in the tarragon. Add any accumulated juices to the sauce. Slice the turkey across the grain and serve with a spoonful of sauce.

*For old-fashioned goodness, this colorful turkey stew with tender baking powder biscuits on top has few peers. It is a wonderful way to celebrate after Thanksgiving with the leftovers from the holiday bird. Although it can serve six, four happy eaters with hearty appetites and good conversation could easily finish it. Change the vegetables to suit your taste and substitute leftover chicken for the turkey, if you prefer.*

Prepare biscuit dough and refrigerate.

Meanwhile, preheat your oven to 450°F. Position the rack in the middle of the oven.

Heat the butter and oil in a deep 10-inch cast-iron skillet or Dutch oven over medium-high heat until hot. Add the carrots, celery, and yellow onion and cook until lightly browned, 5 to 6 minutes. Add the mushrooms and pearl onions and cook, stirring, until the pearl onions are lightly browned, 5 to 6 minutes more.

Stir in the flour and cook until pale golden color, 1 to 2 minutes. Pour in the stock, stir until blended, and bring to a boil, stirring constantly; then reduce the heat and simmer until the sauce thickens, about 3 minutes. Add the turkey and return the liquid to a boil. Stir in the peas, parsley, and thyme, season to taste with salt and pepper, and keep warm over low heat.

*Finish biscuits:* Lightly dust a work surface with flour. Roll out or pat out the dough into a 1/2-inch-thick disc. With a

# Turkey and Biscuits Casserole
## Serves 4 to 6

Turkey Filling
Biscuits (recipe follows)

FILLING:

2 tablespoons unsalted butter

2 tablespoons canola or vegetable oil

2 medium carrots, peeled and diced

1 large stalk celery, trimmed and diced

1 medium yellow onion, peeled and diced

4 ounces white mushrooms, wiped, trimmed and sliced

1 cup frozen pearl onions, defrosted

1/3 cup unbleached all-purpose flour

3 cups+ chicken stock

Salt and freshly ground black pepper

2 tablespoons finely chopped flat-leaf parsley

1 tablespoon fresh thyme leaves or 1 teaspoon dried thyme leaves

1 pound cooked turkey, cut into bite-size pieces (about 4 cups)

1 cup frozen petite peas, defrosted

2 1/2-inch cookie cutter, cut the dough into circles, gathering any extra dough together and re-rolling it. Lay the biscuits over the turkey mixture, carefully brush the tops with milk, and transfer the pot to the oven to bake until the biscuits are golden brown on top, about 23 minutes. Remove and let stand for 10 minutes before serving.

. . . . . . . . . . . . . . . . . . . . . . . . . . . . . . . . . . . . . . . .

## Biscuits

1 ½ cups unbleached all-purpose flour, plus more for dusting

2 teaspoons baking powder

1 teaspoon sugar

½ teaspoon salt

5 tablespoons cold unsalted butter, cut into cubes

½ cup + 2 tablespoons whole milk + milk to brush on the biscuits

Combine the flour, baking powder, sugar, and salt in a food processor fitted with a steel chopping blade and process briefly to blend. Add the butter and pulse until the butter is the size of small peas; then pour in the milk and process just until the dough pulls together. Do not over-process. Remove the dough from the bowl. Pat it into a ball, flatten into 3/4-inch-thick disc, and dust with flour; cover with plastic wrap and refrigerate until ready to use.

# Duck with Apples, Oranges, and Cider

*Serves 4*

*Braised duck with Calvados, cider, and apples recalls the robust fare of Normandy. This version, from tea expert and friend John Harney, includes orange and lemon juice and orange segments in the rich sauce. Although it takes time to slowly render the fat, brown the skin, and simmer the duck until tender, you'll savor a superb dinner or lazy Sunday lunch. Serve the duck over noodles or boiled potatoes. And save the rendered duck fat to make divine oven-roasted or fried potatoes.*

*If French hard cider or fermented fresh cider is unavailable, use good quality apple juice.*

1 (5-pound) duck

1 tablespoon grapeseed or peanut oil

Salt and freshly ground black pepper

1 cup water

2 large sprigs flat-leaf parsley +
   2 tablespoons finely chopped parsley
   to finish the sauce

3 navel oranges, washed

1 lemon, washed
   1 medium yellow onion, peeled and
   finely chopped

3 cloves garlic, peeled and minced

2 cups French-style hard cider or naturally
   fermented, unpasteurized fresh cider

⅓ cup Calvados or other apple brandy

2 tart-sweet, crisp apples

Remove the neck and giblets from the duck's cavity; discard the liver. Rinse the duck under cold water and pat dry. Cut off the wingtips and excess fat and reserve. Using sharp scissors or poultry shears, remove the backbone by cutting along one side and then the other, then cut along the breastbone; divide the duck into leg, thigh, and breast sections. Cut each breast and thigh into 2 parts; blot dry with paper towels. Using a sharp knife, score the duck's skin and fat in small squares, taking care not to cut the flesh. Season both sides with salt and pepper.

Heat a 12- or 13-inch cast-iron skillet over medium heat until hot, about 3 1/2 minutes. Add the oil and duck pieces, skin-side down, and gently sauté them until the skin is a rich brown and the fat under the skin is rendered, about 20 to 30 minutes, pouring off the fat about every 10 minutes. (You do not want the duck to stew in its own fat, or it will become a confit.)

While the duck browns, put a 2-inch piece of duck fat in a medium-sized skillet and heat it over medium-high heat. When fat covers the bottom of the pan, add the giblets, neck, and wingtips and brown the pieces on all sides, about 10 minutes. Add the water and parsley sprigs, turn the heat down, and let the liquid simmer.

With a zester or micro-plane, remove the zest from 2 of the oranges and the lemon and reserve. Squeeze the juice from both fruits. Reserve the third orange.

Once the duck pieces have browned, transfer them to a large bowl; discard all but 1 tablespoon of fat from the cast-iron skillet. Turn the heat to medium-high, add the onion and sauté until golden, 3 to 4 minutes; stir in the garlic and cook for 30 seconds.

Combine the cider and Calvados and pour them into the pan; bring to a boil, stirring up all the browned cooking bits. Strain the liquid from the other skillet and add it along with the orange and lemon juices into the larger skillet, and bring to a boil. Return the duck to the pan and spoon the sauce over the pieces several times. Cover the skillet, turn the heat down so the liquid barely simmers, and cook until the duck is completely tender when pierced with a fork, about 50 minutes. Turn your oven to warm. Put a platter in the oven to heat.

Transfer the duck to the warm platter, tent with aluminum foil, and keep warm.

Over high heat, reduce the pan liquid by half, 20 to 25 minutes. Meanwhile, wash the remaining orange, slice off the top and bottom, and cut it into 8 segments. Peel and core the apples and cut them into 8 segments. Add the apples and orange to the sauce, and continue cooking over medium heat until the apples are just tender, about 5 minutes, turning occasionally. Taste to adjust the seasonings.

Arrange the apples and oranges around the duck on the platter. Stir the 2 tablespoons of chopped parsley into the sauce, and spoon a little of the sauce over the duck. Sprinkle on the grated orange and lemon zests, and serve.

# Aunt Ellen's Delicious Kitchen Tested Dishes

### AUNT ELLEN'S FRIED CHICKEN LOUISIANE

Fry chicken uncovered in two tablespoonfuls of sizzling butter, till each piece is brown. Slice an onion into skillet and let brown; add four shredded green peppers and let them brown. Stir in two tablespoonfuls flour, teaspoonful chopped parsley and pinch of bay leaf. Season with salt, pepper, paprika. Slice in four large tomatoes, or use two cups canned tomatoes. Let chicken simmer under self-basting cover for half hour on cooler part of range. Add one cup water, cover again, let simmer for another half hour. Dish up and garnish with curly slices of bacon.

### AUNT ELLEN'S BRAISED CHICKEN

Stuff a plump pullet with a dressing made of two cupfuls of soft bread crumbs, 1/2 teaspoonful of salt, 1/4 teaspoonful of pepper, a dash of paprika, a teaspoonful each of grated onion and finely chopped parsley with a bit of poultry seasoning; and two tablespoonfuls of butter which you cut into crumbs. Then put the chicken in the Tite-Top Dutch Oven on top of eight slices of sizzling bacon that you have just covered with two chopped carrots, two chopped onions, and five tablespoonfuls of water. Sprinkle the chicken with a tablespoonful of finely chopped parsley and a small bit of bay leaf. Cover it. Let it cook steadily over slow heat for an hour. Then add one cupful of boiling water, one cupful strained tomato juice, half a teaspoonful of salt, and pepper to taste. Cover again, and let chicken cook till tender and brown. Serve on hot platter with crisped bacon or little sausages. Thicken the remaining juices and vegetables to rich gravy.

**WAGNER CAST IRON WARE** now *Pre-Seasoned*

Ready to Use...
NO
BREAKING IN!

Gives the Delicious Flavor of Old Fashioned Cooking

Manufacturing Company, Sidney, Ohio, U. S. A.

# Easy Cassoulet

*Serves 6*

*Cassoulet is a hearty stew from the south of France. It typically contains a variety of sausages and duck along with white haricot beans. I considered it rather time consuming until Haejin Baek prepared this easy version for me with purchased legs of duck confit, canned beans, and a variety of spicy sausages. Even if it takes a couple of hours to cook, Haejin's recipe is easy and the casserole seems only to improve when reheated.*

2 tablespoons olive oil

3 cups chopped yellow onions

2 tablespoons dried basil leaves

6 purchased duck legs confit

3 pounds assorted mixed sausages, such as kielbasa and andouille, sliced into 1-inch pieces, and uncooked garlic-pork sausage, casing removed

3 (15-ounce) cans Great Northern white beans, drained

1 (28-ounce) can whole tomatoes

1 large head garlic (8 to 12 cloves), crushed

3 sprigs fresh thyme or 1 tablespoon dried thyme leaves

3 bay leaves

2 slices French bread, pulsed in a food processor or blender to make bread crumbs

Salt and freshly ground black pepper

Preheat your oven to 325°F.

Heat a large cast-iron Dutch oven over medium-high heat until hot but not smoking, 3 1/2 to 4 minutes. Add the oil, onions, and basil and sauté until the onions are soft, about 5 minutes. Turn the temperature to low.

Meanwhile, heat a large cast-iron skillet over medium-high heat until hot, about 3 minutes. Add the duck legs, and cook to render off as much fat as possible, turning once or twice, 3 to 5 minutes; transfer them to the pot with the onions. Discard all but 1 tablespoon of the fat from the skillet. Add the uncooked sausage meat and sauté until it is almost cooked through, breaking it into pieces with a wooden spatula, and then add it to the Dutch oven.

Put the sliced cooked sausages in the skillet and sauté until some of the fat is rendered. Add them to the Dutch oven along with the beans, tomatoes, garlic, thyme, and bay leaves;

stir gently to mix. Cover the pot and transfer to the oven to bake.

After about 1 1/2 to 2 hours, when the duck meat easily pulls off the bone, remove the pot from the oven and stir gently; season to taste with salt and pepper. Turn the heat down to 300°, sprinkle the bread crumbs on top, and return the pot uncovered to the oven for another 30 minutes.

MEAT

"The secret of good cooking is largely a matter of developing and enhancing the natural food flavors which the Griswold Dutch Oven does so well, because it retains the steam and conserves the natural juices of all foods cooked."

–Aunt Ellen

# Stuffed Peppers with Moroccan Lamb

## *Serves 4*

Canola or vegetable oil

4 large bell peppers (any color)

1 pound ground lamb

1/2 cup uncooked couscous

1/2 cup drained canned plum tomatoes, finely chopped

1/3 cup finely chopped pitted prunes

1/4 cup slivered blanched almonds, toasted in a 350 °F oven until lightly browned

2 cloves garlic, peeled and minced

1 small yellow onion, peeled and finely chopped

2 tablespoons chopped cilantro leaves + chopped leaves to garnish

1 1/2 teaspoons salt

1 teaspoon ground cumin

1 teaspoon ground ginger

1/2 teaspoon freshly ground black pepper

1/8 teaspoon cayenne

Cucumber-Yogurt-Mint Sauce, optional (recipe follows)

*Stuffed peppers have been a staple in American kitchens for generations, and many nationalities have put their own imprint or flavorings on the homey dish. This version was inspired by Middle Eastern lamb dishes where the meat is often seasoned with an aromatic blend of sweet and savory ingredients and spices. Rather than using rice in the mixture, I added couscous. You might also substitute ground beef or turkey for the lamb. Although a sauce is not necessary, thick Middle Eastern yogurt mixed with chopped fresh mint and diced cucumbers is delicious.*

Lightly brush a deep cast-iron skillet large enough to hold the peppers in a single layer with oil. Preheat your oven to 350°F.

Slice the tops off the peppers (about 3/4-inch down), and set them aside. Remove the seeds and membranes; if necessary, cut a very thin slice from the bottom of each pepper so they stand level.

In a bowl, mix together the lamb, couscous, tomatoes, prunes, almonds, garlic, onion, cilantro, salt, cumin, ginger, and black and cayenne peppers. Fill the peppers, replace the tops, and brush them with oil.

Put the peppers in the skillet, cover loosely with foil, and bake until the lamb is cooked through, the peppers are tender, and the skin starts to brown, 60 to 75 minutes, depending on how

thick the walls of the peppers are. Remove the tops and run the peppers under the broiler to lightly brown the meat, about 5 minutes. Remove the skillet, re-cover the peppers, and let them stand for at least 10 minutes. Sprinkle with the chopped cilantro, and serve with Cucumber-Yogurt-Mint Sauce, if desired.

. . . . . . . . . . . . . . . . . . . . . . . . . . . . . . . . . .

## Cucumber-Yogurt-Mint Sauce

1 small cucumber, peeled, seeded, and finely diced

1 cup thick Middle Eastern–style plain yogurt

Salt and freshly ground black pepper

Chopped mint leaves, to garnish

In a small bowl, combine the cucumber, yogurt, and salt and pepper to taste. Add the mint and drizzle the sauce over the stuffed peppers.

# Provençal Lamb Stew

*Serves 6*

2 tablespoons olive oil

3 pounds lamb shoulder chops, about
  1-inch thick, blotted dry (about 6)

Salt and freshly ground black pepper

1 large yellow onion, peeled and thinly
  sliced crosswise

1 each red and green bell peppers, seeds
  and membranes removed, and chopped

2 large cloves garlic, peeled and finely
  chopped

1 cup beef stock

1 (14-ounce) can imported Italian
  tomatoes, undrained and coarsely
  chopped

1 rosemary sprig + sprigs for garnish

2 medium zucchini, cut in half lengthwise
  and sliced

1 small eggplant, peeled and diced

½ pound boiling potatoes, preferably
  yellow, peeled and diced

¼ cup pitted small oil-cured black olives

¼ cup julienned fresh basil leaves or finely
  chopped flat-leaf parsley

*The sunny flavors and colors in this rustic stew remind me of dishes in the south of France. Like many stews, this one can be made ahead and reheated, and the flavors will improve. Add the basil or parsley just before serving, and bring a loaf of crusty French bread to the table for soaking up the sauce.*

*I leave the bones in the shoulder chops because I love to nibble on them; I also think they keep the meat juicier. If you prefer, remove the bones before serving or use about 2 pounds of lamb stew meat.*

Preheat your oven to 350°F.

Season the lamb chops generously with salt and pepper. Heat a 10-inch cast-iron Dutch oven over high heat until hot but not smoking, 3 1/2 to 4 minutes  Add the oil and the lamb chops, two at a time, and brown them on all sides, turning to color evenly, 3 to 4 minutes each side; remove to a bowl and continue with the remaining chops. Once all the chops are browned, trim off the large pieces of fat and discard.

If the oil has burned, discard it, wipe out the skillet, and add another tablespoon of oil. Stir in the onions and peppers and sauté them over medium-high heat until the onions are golden, 3 to 4 minutes. Stir in the garlic and cook for 30 seconds. Pour in the stock and stir up any browned bits. Add the tomatoes and rosemary, return the lamb to the pot and

bring to a boil; cover and transfer the pot to the oven to cook until the meat is almost fork-tender, about 1 hour.

Remove the pot from the oven. Add the zucchini, eggplant, and potatoes, and return it uncovered to the oven, and cook until the vegetables are tender, about 1/2 hour. Stir in the olives and basil or parsley, taste to adjust the seasonings, and serve on plates or in flat bowls garnished with small sprigs of rosemary.

# AUNT ELLEN'S SECRETS ABOUT CUTS OF MEAT

| *1 Neck | *6 Brisket | *12 Rump |
| *2 Chuck | 7 Cross Ribs | 13 Round |
| 3 Ribs | *8 Plate | 14 Second Cut |
| *4 Shoulder Clod | *9 Navel | Round |
| *5 Fore Shank | 10 Loin | *15 Hind Shank |
| | *11 Flank | |

*Stars and shaded areas indicate less expensive cuts of beef.

Every good housewife knows that the prices of many meats are based largely on their demand and appearance. Many of the less expensive cuts of meat have greater food value; and this booklet is intended to help you in knowing how to buy and prepare them.

*Beef Short Ribs*

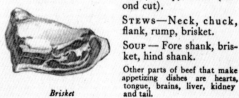

*Brisket*

## CERTAIN CUTS ARE ADAPTED TO CERTAIN DISHES

STEAKS — Loin, flank, round, shoulder clod.

ROASTS — Ribs, loin, flank.

POT ROASTS — Neck, shoulder clod, chuck, flank, rump, round (second cut).

STEWS — Neck, chuck, flank, rump, brisket.

SOUP — Fore shank, brisket, hind shank.

Other parts of beef that make appetizing dishes are hearts, tongue, brains, liver, kidney and tail.

12

# CUTS OF LAMB AND MUTTON

| *1 Neck | *3 Shoulder | 5 Loin |
| *2 Chuck | *4 Flank | 6 Leg |

*Stars and shaded areas indicate the less expensive cuts of lamb.

The relative difference in food value between lamb and mutton is the same as between veal and beef. The mature meat is more nutritious, but has a less delicate flavor. Folks who know, eliminate the strong flavor of mutton, objectionable to many, by removing the outside fat and skin before cooking.

You may consider lamb and mutton as expensive, because perhaps, you buy only chops and roasts. But you will find the cheaper cuts will make delicious dishes in a variety that will be enjoyed.

The Griswold Tite-Top Dutch Oven is invaluable in cooking these meats, since so many cuts require a slow simmering process with even heat on all sides.

## GENERAL COOKING CLASSIFICATIONS

*Shoulder*

CHOPS—Loin and ribs.

ROASTS—Shoulder, flank, chuck and leg.

STEWS—Flank, shoulder, chuck and neck.

BROTH—Neck.

13

# Sicilian Orange Beef Stew

*Serves 6*

*Chef Joe DiMaggio, Jr. is a distant cousin of the baseball great but no less a star. My friend Joe travels the world as a consultant to restaurants. His tangy-sweet stew reflects his Sicilian ancestry. Sicily is famous for, among other things, the combination of sweet and savory flavors that early Arabs brought to the island. Joe hits a homer with this dish. Serve it over polenta or Cheesy Stone-Ground Grits (page 78).*

2 to 4 tablespoons olive oil

2 pounds beef chuck or prime rib, cut into 1 ½-inch cubes and blotted dry

Salt and freshly ground black pepper

1 pound pearl onions, peeled with an "x" cut in the root end of each onion or 12 ounces defrosted frozen pearl onions (about 2 cups), blotted dry

2 large cloves garlic, peeled and halved

¾ teaspoon ground cloves

¾ teaspoon ground cumin

½ teaspoon cinnamon

½ cup tomato sauce

1 ¾ cups full-bodied red wine, such as merlot or cabernet sauvignon

Juice (about 1 cup) and grated zest of 2 large oranges (keep zest separate)

⅓ cup defrosted frozen orange juice concentrate with pulp

3 bay leaves

Preheat your oven to 325°F.

Heat a 10-inch cast-iron Dutch oven with lid over high heat until hot but not smoking, 3 1/2 to 4 minutes. Add half of the oil and the meat in batches and brown on all sides, taking care not to crowd the pan. Remove the pieces to a large bowl as they are browned and when all the pieces are browned, season them with about 1/4 teaspoon salt and pepper.

If the oil has burned, discard it, wipe out the pot, and add the remaining oil. Stir in the pearl onions, reduce the heat to medium, and sauté until they begin to brown, 4 to 5 minutes, shaking the pan often. Or, add the defrosted pearl onions and brown over medium-high heat, shaking the pan frequently, 2 or 3 minutes, until browned. Add the garlic and cook for 30 seconds; then stir in the cloves, cumin, cinnamon, tomato sauce, salt, and pepper. Pour in the wine, stirring to scrape up any browned bits from the bottom of the pan; add the orange juice, the orange juice concentrate, and the bay leaves. Return the meat to the pot, bring it to a boil, cover, and transfer to the oven to cook for 1 hour.

Remove the lid and continue cooking the stew for an additional hour, stirring a few times, or until the meat is very tender. Discard the bay leaves and, if the sauce is too thin, reduce the liquid over high heat on top of the stove, about 5 minutes. Stir in the orange zest, season to taste with salt and pepper, and serve.

# Vintage Beef Stew

*Serves 6*

3 tablespoons canola or vegetable oil

2 pounds beef chuck, cut in 1 ½-inch cubes, blotted dry

1 large yellow onion, peeled and sliced crosswise

1 large clove garlic, peeled and sliced

4 cups boiling water + ½ cup cold water

1 tablespoon salt

1 tablespoon freshly squeezed lemon juice

1 teaspoon sugar

1 teaspoon Worcestershire sauce

½ teaspoon freshly ground black pepper

½ teaspoon paprika

1 to 2 bay leaves

4 cloves

Dash allspice

6 carrots, peeled and cut crosswise in 4 pieces; halved lengthwise, if thick

3 to 4 boiling potatoes, peeled and cut into medium chunks

12 ounces frozen pearl onions (2 cups) defrosted and blotted dry

4 tablespoons cornstarch

*This homey recipe was given to my friend Sarah Collins by her mother, Elizabeth French, who called it "Man Size Stew." But Sarah remembers that everyone in her family—not just her dad—loved it, so she renamed it Vintage Beef Stew because flavorful home cooking appeals to almost all of us. If time is short, the beef can be braised separately, refrigerated in its broth, and reheated later when you can add the vegetables to finish the stew.*

Heat 2 tablespoons of the oil in a large cast-iron Dutch oven over high heat until very hot. Add the beef and brown on all sides, about 20 minutes. Do this in batches if using a 10-inch or smaller pot, removing the pieces to a bowl as they are cooked. When all of the beef is browned, return it to the pot, along with the sliced onion, garlic, boiling water, and all the ingredients through the allspice; cover and simmer for at least 2 hours, stirring occasionally. The meat should be almost tender.

Add the carrots and potatoes and simmer for 30 to 40 minutes longer or until everything is very tender, adding a little water if everything is not about two-thirds covered. Meanwhile, heat the remaining oil in a medium skillet over medium-high heat. Add the pearl onions and sauté until they are lightly browned, 4 to 5 minutes, shaking the pan frequently. Discard the bay leaf and cloves and stir the pearl onions into the pot.

In a small jar, combine the cornstarch and the 1/2 cup of cold water, and shake hard to blend. Pour the liquid into the pot and heat to a simmer, stirring until the gravy thickens. Cook gently for a few minutes longer and serve.

# Mammy Lape's Roast Beef

*Serves 8*

1 (4 ½-pound) piece beef chuck about 2 to 2 ½ inches thick, tied

Unbleached all-purpose flour, for dredging, + ¼ cup flour for the gravy

¼ teaspoon salt

1 teaspoon freshly ground black pepper

2 tablespoons olive oil

2 stalks celery, trimmed and coarsely chopped

1 large yellow onion, peeled and quartered

1 medium carrot, peeled and coarsely chopped

2 ¼ cups chicken or beef stock

1 cup whole milk

*I always thought roast beef was the prime ribs my mom made for special occasions. The meat was carved at the table and served medium-rare with potatoes roasted in the drippings. That's not what my Ohio-born husband thought, as I found out when his daughter Debbie sent me this version of her grandmother's roast beef, where a large piece of chuck is seared in a Dutch oven and cooked with a few aromatic vegetables for five hours. Milk gravy seems to be Dutch or German, as well as Southern. It's made with pan drippings thickened with flour and milk.*

*It's not the prime ribs of my youth, but judging by the enthusiastic reaction the dish gets when we serve it, it's a sentimental winner. I like to break the cooked meat into chunks and return them to the sauce, because they are more succulent that way. Serve with noodles or mashed potatoes.*

Preheat your oven to 325°F.

Flour all sides of the meat, patting to remove the excess, and season with salt and pepper. Heat a 10-inch cast-iron Dutch oven over high heat until hot but not smoking, 3 1/2 to 4 minutes. Add the oil and the beef and sear the meat well on all sides.

Add the celery, onion, and carrot but no liquid. (The pan juices will provide enough moisture.) Cover the pot and place it the oven for 5 hours, turning the meat once after 2 1/2 hours. Remove from the oven and transfer the meat to a bowl or platter. At this point, you can let it cool and remove any fat or simply finish the sauce and serve.

With a slotted spoon, transfer the vegetables to a food processor and process until smooth; return them to the pan along with the stock. Combine the milk and remaining 1/4 cup of flour in a small jar and shake vigorously to mix. Bring the liquid to a boil and add as much of the milk mixture as needed to thicken the gravy to the right consistency, starting with about three-quarters of the mixture. Taste to adjust the seasonings.

Cut the meat in slices and serve it with the gravy spooned over it on the plate. Or break it into chunks and return the meat to the gravy to simmer. Serve over noodles or mashed potatoes.

# All-American Short Ribs

*Serves 4*

In many upscale restaurants, bony, tough short ribs are being braised until fall-off-the-bone tender and served as stylish entrées. In my Southern-inspired version, the cooking liquid includes aromatic vegetables, stock, and tomatoes along with bourbon and molasses. (I like the robust, slightly less sweet taste of dark molasses, but you can also use the light variety.) You can make these several days ahead and refrigerate them, then slowly reheat before serving. Serve them over Cheesy Stone-Ground Grits (page 78) or mashed potatoes.

Short ribs are generally sold in 1- and 2-inch lengths. I think the shorter ones are easier to work with, but with either size, you should figure about a pound of uncooked ribs per person.

4 pounds bone-in beef short ribs, blotted dry

Salt and freshly ground black pepper

2 tablespoons grapeseed or canola oil

2 medium carrots, peeled and diced

1 medium yellow onion, peeled and diced

1 large stalk celery, trimmed and diced

1 tablespoon finely chopped garlic

½ cup bourbon

1 ½ cups beef stock

1 (14-ounce) can diced tomatoes, undrained

½ cup dark or light molasses

3 large sprigs fresh thyme or 1 tablespoon dried leaves

2 bay leaves

2 tablespoons chopped flat-leaf parsley, to garnish

Preheat your oven to 350°F. Season the short ribs with the salt and pepper. Heat a large cast-iron Dutch oven over high heat until hot but not smoking, 3 1/2 to 4 minutes. Pour in about 1 tablespoon of the oil and, working in batches, add as many ribs as can fit comfortably in the bottom of the pan without crowding; sear them on all sides. Remove the browned ribs to a large bowl, adding oil as needed, and continue until all the ribs are cooked, 15 to 20 minutes total cooking time if done in batches.

Drain all but 1 tablespoon of fat from the pan. Stir in the carrots, onion, and celery and sauté over medium-high heat until lightly browned, about 5 minutes, stirring often. Stir in the garlic, cook for 30 seconds, then pour in the bourbon and boil over high heat until almost evaporated, 1 1/2 minutes. Add the stock, tomatoes, molasses, thyme sprigs, and bay

leaves; return the ribs to the pot and bring to a boil. Cover the pot and transfer it to the oven to braise until the meat is fork-tender, 1 1/2 to 2 hours.

Remove the pot from the oven. Using tongs, transfer the short ribs to a bowl. Pour the liquid through a strainer into a fat separator. Return the meat and strained vegetables to the pot, cover, and set aside. Once the liquid has separated, discard the fat, and stir the liquid into the pot. If the sauce is too thin, gently boil to reduce and slightly thicken it, spooning it over the ribs and turning them occasionally. Season to taste with salt and pepper. Discard the bay leaves and thyme stems, sprinkle with parsley, and serve. Alternatively, cover and refrigerate the pot overnight or until the fat congeals, then scrape off the fat and continue with the recipe.

# Things Every Housewife Should Know

**She must learn the art of cooking** so that she can prepare appetizing dishes from meat and vegetables and combine both so as to only have to add a small quantity of meat and the cheaper cuts at that. Any dish well-cooked, attractively garnished, and served will please the eye and stimulate the appetite, the most humble, simple dish very often being turned into a meal out of the commonplace. In cooking the cheaper the cuts of meat that have little fat, such as round, rump, etc., they should have fat added when cooking.

When buying meat the housewife must remember in considering the piece of meat, the amount of fat, bone, gristle and so forth, must be studied. If some of the cheaper cuts have more bone and fat she must insist on her butcher giving her what belongs to her; after the butcher weighs the meat he often trims a great deal of bone and fat off, the housewife has paid for these parts and should take them home with her. The fat may be fried out and kept for different purposes for cooking, lamb fat which is not good for cooking should be fried out and saved for soap making. The bones may all be used for soup.

When beef is first cut it is dark purple, this turning to red on exposure to air. Fresh beef has a heavy layer of crumbly fat on the outside, the color being yellowish white, the fat on the inside is the white. Good beef has a great deal of fat and very little water. The fat of old beef is hard and skinny, the lean part being dark red.

If the housewife does not know the different cuts of meat her butcher has her at a great disadvantage, but let her know how to buy and insist on getting what she asks for and much money can be saved.

—*The Comfort Food Cookbook*, circa 1925

# Korean Braised Short Ribs (Kalbi-jim)

*Serves 6*

Among her friends, Haejin Baek, a New York banker, is popular for her spectacular dinner parties, often with the Korean foods she grew up with in Seoul. Her succulent, aromatic short ribs in the Korean style are some of the best I have had. Haejin trims much of the fat off the face of each short rib before searing them. The fork-tender ribs can be cooked ahead of time and reheated.

1 tablespoon canola or vegetable oil

Salt and freshly ground black pepper

5 to 6 pounds bone-in beef short ribs, blotted dry

1 cup soy sauce

1/2 cup sake

1/4 cup mirin

1/4 cup toasted sesame oil

1/4 cup sesame seeds

2 teaspoons dried red chile flakes

2 teaspoons freshly ground black pepper

2 bunches scallions, including most of the green parts, chopped

1 head garlic (8 to 12 cloves) peeled and crushed or chopped

1 tablespoon minced ginger root

2 cups water

2 or 3 small or 1 large boiling potato

2 large carrots

2 medium onions

3 cups boiled rice, as accompaniment

Preheat your oven to 350°F.

Heat a large cast-iron Dutch oven over medium-high heat until hot but not smoking, 3 1/2 to 4 minutes. Add oil to cover the bottom of the pan and as many short ribs as will fit in comfortably without crowding; sear them until browned on all sides. With metal tongs, remove the ribs to a bowl and continue with the remaining ribs, adding more oil, if needed, until all the ribs are browned.

Return the ribs to the pot. Add the soy sauce, sake, mirin, sesame oil, sesame seeds, chile flakes, black pepper, scallions, garlic, ginger, and water and bring to a boil. Cover the pot and transfer it to the oven to cook until the meat is almost tender, 1 1/2 to 2 hours.

Shortly before the short ribs are done, peel and cut the potatoes, carrots, and onions into 1-inch chunks. Once the meat is tender, add the vegetables to the pot and gently stir. Cook another 30 to 45 minutes until the vegetables are tender and the meat begins to fall off the bones.

Remove the pot from the oven and cool slightly; strain the liquid into a fat strainer. Return the meat and vegetables to the pot, cover, and set aside until the liquid is separated. Discard the fat; return the liquid into the pot, and gently boil to reduce and slightly thicken the gravy, 15 to 30 minutes. Serve with rice. Alternatively, cover and refrigerate the pot overnight or until the fat congeals, then scrape off the fat and continue with the recipe.

# Steak 'n' Stout with Glazed Onions

*Serves 2*

*I love steak that is crunchy on the outside and deep pink inside. While the steak sears in your grill pan, the stout-brown sugar marinade reduces over mounds of sautéed onions into a caramelized glaze. Served together, they are a sublime treat. This recipe is easily doubled.*

6 ounces (¾ cup) stout or dark beer

2 tablespoons firmly packed dark brown sugar

1 tablespoon cider vinegar

1 clove garlic, peeled and split

1 bay leaf

1 ¼ to 1 ½ pounds bone-in shell steak or porterhouse steak, 1 ¼ inches thick

1 ½ tablespoons unsalted butter

1 teaspoon vegetable oil

2 large yellow onions, peeled and thinly sliced

Salt and freshly ground black pepper to taste

Combine the stout, brown sugar, vinegar, garlic, and bay leaf in a resealable plastic bag; add the steak and let it sit for at least 1 hour, turning after 1/2 hour. (The meat may marinate for several hours.)

In the meantime, melt the butter and oil in a large skillet over medium-high heat. Add the onions and sauté them until golden brown, 12 to 15 minutes, stirring often. Set aside.

Heat a cast-iron grill pan or griddle over high heat for at least 5 minutes. When very hot, remove the steak from the marinade, blot it dry, and cook the first side for 6 to 7 minutes. Turn and cook the other side for 5 to 6 minutes for medium-rare.

While the steak is cooking, pour 1/2 cup of the marinade onto the onions, turn the heat to high, and boil until the liquid evaporates, stirring often, 6 to 8 minutes. Season with salt and pepper to taste and keep warm.

Transfer the steak to a slicing board, season with salt and pepper, and let it rest for 3 to 5 minutes. Slice across the grain and serve with the onions on top or under the meat slices.

# Aunt Ellen's Delicious Kitchen Tested Dishes

## ❈ ❈
## AUNT ELLEN'S MOCK DUCK

Score till rough, one side of large thin round steak. Melt 1 tablespoon of butter in skillet, drop in 1 finely chopped onion, chopped sprig of parsley, and brown. Add 1 1/2 cups of soft bread crumbs, 1/2 teaspoon salt, and sprinkling each of pepper, paprika and sage. Spread this dressing thickly over steak, roll compactly, tie, flour, and sear in your Tite-Top Dutch Oven rubbed with suet. When brown, add 1 tablespoon of vinegar, cover tightly, and let simmer for 1 1/2 hours. If necessary, add 1/2 cup of boiling water in 1/2 hour, and season with salt and pepper. When done, make gravy by adding 1/2 cup boiling water or liquid from canned tomatoes, 1/2 teaspoon Worcestershire sauce, and one tablespoon flour mixed with three of cold water. Boil, season and strain.

❈ ❈

## ❈ ❈
## AUNT ELLEN'S SWISS STEAK

This is an inexpensive round steak made wonderfully delicious! To make it, pound flour into about two and a half pounds of the round cut thick. Pound in all it will take, a whole cupful if possible; and use the rim of a stout saucer so you won't break up the fibers of the meat. Then lay the steak on two or three slices of sizzling bacon in a skillet, pour half a cup of hot water, stock, or tomato juice around it, drop in a medium sized onion in which you have placed one clove, add the tiniest bit of bay leaf...use self-basting cover on skillet and let the steak simmer for an hour. Then mix one-fourth teaspoonful of dry mustard in one-half cupful of water or tomato juice, pour it into the skillet, dash in a little celery, salt and a tablespoonful of walnut or tomato catsup, and let the meat simmer under cover for a half hour or an hour longer... when it will be tender, savory, and ready to serve. For gravy, simply strain the juices that are around this steak...no additional thickening or seasoning is necessary.

❈ ❈

# Nona's Italian Meatloaf

*Serves 3 to 4*

*Among traditional comfort foods, meatloaf is a clear favorite. Southern cooks have made them in cast-iron skillets for generations, usually baked in the oven. But my friend Bobby D'Angelo, a chef, told me that his grandmother Nora La Rose cooked hers in a skillet. As a seamstress raising two daughters alone, with minimal time, she put the meat mixture together in the morning and cooked it on the stovetop when she got home. It took about 35 minutes. Nora used Crisco, but vegetable oil also works. The pan gravy is delicious. Serve with noodles or mashed potatoes.*

6 slices day-old Italian bread including crust, about 1-inch thick

1 cup milk

1 large egg

1 pound lean ground beef (about 20 percent fat)

1 cup (4 ounces) grated Parmigiano-Reggiano cheese

1 small yellow onion, peeled and grated, divided

2 tablespoons finely chopped flat-leaf parsley

1 teaspoon dried oregano

1 teaspoon salt

1/2 teaspoon freshly ground black pepper

2 tablespoons Crisco or other solid vegetable shortening, or vegetable oil

1 cup beef or chicken stock

2 tablespoons unbleached all-purpose flour

8 ounces white mushrooms, trimmed, wiped, and quartered, if large; cut in half, if small

1 tablespoon Worcestershire sauce

Soak the bread in the milk until soft, about 5 minutes, and squeeze dry. In a large mixing bowl, beat the egg, then add the beef, bread, cheese, half of the onion, the parsley, oregano, salt, and pepper. Form the mixture into a loaf about 7 x 4 x 2 inches high; cover, and chill for at least 1 hour but preferably for 8 hours or overnight.

Heat the shortening in a 12-inch cast-iron skillet over medium-high heat until hot but not smoking, 3 1/2 to 4 minutes. Put the meatloaf in the center of the pan and cook until browned, about 4 minutes. Using a spatula, carefully turn the meatloaf and brown the other side; then remove it to a plate.

Discard all but 2 tablespoons of fat. Over medium-high heat, stir the flour into the pan and cook until browed. Pour in the stock and bring to a boil, scraping up any browned cooking bits. Stir in the remaining onion, the mushrooms, and the

Worcestershire sauce; then return the meatloaf to the pan, cover tightly, and cook over low heat for about 30 minutes. Remove the meatloaf from the pan, let it stand for about 5 minutes, then slice and serve with the gravy.

# My Favorite Chili

*Serves 6 to 8*

3 tablespoons canola or vegetable oil

1 large yellow onion, peeled and finely chopped

1 large green bell pepper, seeds and membranes removed, and chopped

2 large cloves garlic, peeled and minced

1 to 2 jalapeño peppers, seeds and membranes removed, and minced

1 ¼ pounds well-trimmed beef round or venison, cut into ½-inch cubes

¾ pound ground pork

1 (28-ounce) can crushed Italian tomatoes

3 tablespoons ground chili powder, or to taste

2 tablespoons ground cumin

2 tablespoons Worcestershire sauce

2 teaspoons red wine vinegar

½ teaspoon cayenne, or to taste

2 teaspoons salt, or to taste

Freshly ground black pepper

1 (10-ounce) can red kidney beans, rinsed and drained

3 tablespoons masa harina or fine cornmeal, mixed with a little water into a smooth paste (see note)

1 bunch scallions, trimmed and sliced cross-wise, including most of the green parts

*I've been making Southwestern chili since my kids were young. They liked it over baked potatoes with Cheddar cheese. It's also terrific over rice or with Mini Cast-Iron Skillet Cornbread (page 58). I used to make it in huge quantities—sometimes with venison or other game meats—and then froze it in serving-size portions that I defrosted in the microwave.*

*If you like smoky flavors, add some chipotle chili powder along with the traditional chili powder. I also like to add corn kernels and pickled jalapeños.*

Heat a large cast-iron Dutch oven over medium heat until hot but not smoking, 3 1/2 to 4 minutes. Add the oil and stir in the onion, bell pepper, garlic, and jalapeños; cook, stirring occasionally, until the onion is tender, 3 to 4 minutes. Add the cubed and ground meat and continue cooking until the pork is no longer pink, 4 to 5 minutes, breaking the pork into small pieces with a wooden spatula. Stir in the tomatoes, chili powder, cumin, Worcestershire sauce, vinegar, cayenne, and salt and pepper to taste.

Bring the mixture to a boil, then reduce the heat to medium-low and continue to cook the chili uncovered until the meat is tender, 45 minutes to an hour, stirring occasionally. The stew should be fairly thick. Stir in the kidney beans and *masa harina*, if using, and heat through. Taste to adjust the seasonings. Serve garnished with sliced scallions.

*Note:* If your market does not have *masa harina* or cornmeal with the Mexican foods or other flours, the chili may be thickened by cooking it longer over medium heat, stirring it occasionally.

Growing up in Los Angeles, we ate a lot of Tex-Mex food. A friend of my mom's—we called her Aunt Peggy—served a cornbread-topped casserole with spicy meat, beans, cheese, olives, and raisins at her patio parties. I've carried the memory of her tamale pie from my childhood. Judging by online bloggers, countless other people love the dish. I updated it with some authentic ingredients that probably weren't available back then, like chipotles in adobo, mole sauce, and masa harina for tamales, that are now found in many supermarkets and Latino grocery stores.

Tamale pie can be made with ground beef or turkey, pulled pork, purchased or homemade chili, or even as a vegetarian dish with a variety of beans. For game hunters, it's a natural with venison, buffalo, or boar. I love the toothsome quality of the cornmeal topping with corn kernels, but if you are in a hurry, polenta or cornbread mix will also work. Peggy's version had cornbread on the top and bottom, but I prefer it only as a topping.

Heat a 10-inch cast-iron Dutch oven over medium-high heat until just hot, about 3 minutes. Add the oil and onion and sauté until the onion is golden, 3 minutes. Stir in the garlic, cook for 30 seconds, then add the meat and cook until browned on all sides, about 5 minutes, breaking up the pieces with a wooden spatula. Using a large spoon, tip the pan and remove all but about 1 tablespoon of the fat.

# Tamale Pie

## *Serves 8*

Tamale Filling
Cornbread topping (recipe follows)

### FILLING:

1 tablespoon canola or vegetable oil

1 medium yellow onion, peeled and chopped

3 large cloves garlic, peeled and minced

1 ½ pounds lean ground beef

1 green bell pepper, seeds and membranes removed, and chopped

1 (15 ½-ounce) can black beans, rinsed and drained

1 (14 ½-ounce) can diced tomatoes, undrained

2 canned chipotle chiles in adobo sauce, chopped + 1 teaspoon of the adobo sauce from the can, or to taste

2 tablespoon purchased mole paste

1 tablespoon ground cumin

½ cup sliced green or black olives

½ cup golden raisins

Salt and freshly ground black pepper

½ cup chopped cilantro leaves

1 ½ cups (6 ounces) shredded sharp Cheddar cheese, divided

Add the green pepper, tomatoes, chipotle chiles, adobo sauce, mole and cumin; bring to a boil, stirring to blend. Stir in the olives, raisins, about 1 teaspoon of salt, or to taste, and plenty of pepper. Stir in the cilantro and 1 cup of the cheese. Keep the filling warm as you prepare the topping. Preheat your oven to 375°F.

When the cornbread batter is ready, spread it over the meat using a large spoon. Cover the surface and smooth the top with a slightly wet metal spatula or even your fingers.

Bake for 30 minutes, then sprinkle on the remaining cheese and return the pie to the oven. Bake until the top is lightly browned, a toothpick inserted into the crust comes out clean, and the filling is bubbling up on the sides, 10 to 15 minutes. Remove from the oven and let it stand for at least 10 minutes before serving with a large spoon.

## Cornbread topping

1 cup + 2 tablespoons masa harina for tamales or coarse stone-ground cornmeal

½ cup unbleached all-purpose flour

2 tablespoons sugar

1 tablespoon baking powder

1 teaspoon salt

1 ½ cups buttermilk

2 large eggs, beaten

¾ cup defrosted frozen or canned corn kernels, drained

2 tablespoons unsalted butter, melted

In a large bowl, combine the masa harina, flour, sugar, baking powder, and salt. In a small bowl, combine the buttermilk and eggs; stir them into the dry ingredients until blended. Add the corn and butter and mix well.

# Pork Fajitas

*Serves 4*

1 pound pork tenderloin, blotted dry

2 teaspoons ground cumin

1 ½ teaspoons ground chili powder

1 teaspoon ground coriander

½ teaspoon dried oregano

Pinch of cayenne

2 ½ tablespoons olive oil

1 teaspoon salt

Freshly ground black pepper

1 medium yellow onion, peeled and thinly sliced from top to bottom

1 each red and green bell pepper, seeds and membranes removed, and thinly sliced lengthwise

2 large cloves garlic, peeled and minced

1 small jalapeño pepper, seeds and membranes removed, and minced

Juice of 1 lime

8 (8-inch) flour tortillas, warmed in the microwave with a piece of paper towel on top

Garnishes: shredded iceberg lettuce, 1 finely chopped tomato, 1 sliced avocado or ¾ cup guacamole, ¾ cup shredded Cheddar cheese, sour cream, etc.

*Fajitas are easy and fast to make, yet they deliver tons of flavor and satisfaction. Pork tenderloins live up to their name: you don't have to marinate them, as you might with beef flank steak, to be able to cut the meat with a fork. Use about 1 1/2 tablespoons of purchased fajita seasoning or make your own, as I do below, then let everyone garnish their own fajitas at the table.*

Slice the pork tenderloin diagonally into 1/2-inch slices, cut each slice in half lengthwise, and blot dry.

In a small bowl, combine the cumin, chili powder, coriander, oregano, and cayenne.

Heat a 12-inch cast-iron skillet over high heat until very hot and starting to smoke, about 4 minutes. Add 2 tablespoons of the oil and the meat and sauté for 1 1/2 minutes, turning to brown on all sides; season with the salt and pepper to taste.

Add the remaining 1/2 tablespoon of oil, the onion, peppers, garlic, jalapeño, and the seasonings, and cook until the vegetables are crisp-tender, about 2 minutes, stirring often. Pour in the lime juice, scrape up any browned bits on the bottom of the pan, and cook for 1 to 2 minutes more. Taste to adjust the seasonings. Divide the meat among the tortillas, roll up, and serve with the garnishes on the side.

# That delicious smell
## of Home Cooking!

"WHAT are we having for dinner? My, doesn't it smell good!"

How often that delicious smell of home cooking comes from something fried! The ideal way to fry is in a Griswold cast iron skillet because, being iron, it stays heated to the right temperature and keeps your fat really hot with very little fuel.

To have healthful fried meat you must sear the surface quickly, to keep in the good nourishing juices (only very hot fat will do this) and prevent it from soaking up fat and becoming greasy.

Griswold skillets are made of uniformly thick cast iron which distributes the heat evenly, browning the contents just the same all over. In all sizes, from small ones, $4\frac{3}{4}$ inches across the bottom, to large ones, $13\frac{1}{2}$ inches in diameter. Every well-equipped kitchen needs three or four sizes at least.

Griswold cast iron kitchen utensils are carried by all the better stores. If you cannot get them, write direct to us.

**THE GRISWOLD MFG. CO., Dept. K-2, Erie, Penna., U.S.A.**

*Makers of the Bolo Oven, Extra Finished Iron Kitchen Ware, Waffle Irons, Cast Aluminum Cooking Utensils, Food Choppers, Reversible Dampers and Gas Hot Plates*

GRISWOLD

Trade Mark
Reg. U. S. Pat. Off.

# Pan-Seared Pork Chops

*Serves 4*

*These pork chops are very flavorful and juicy. Once you make the Southern Seasoning Mix (or use a purchased rub) they take just minutes to cook. Top them with the Oven-Roasted Wild Mushrooms (page 73) or sautéed onions, or serve them au naturel with mashed potatoes. Store any remaining rub in a small covered jar in a cool, dark place. The blend is great for seasoning Southern Fried Catfish (page 162).*

Oven-Roasted Wild Mushrooms (page 73)

Southern Seasoning Mix (recipe follows)

4 (1-inch thick) bone-in loin pork chops, blotted dry

½ tablespoon canola or olive oil

Salt to taste

Prepare the mushrooms and keep warm, if serving. Prepare the seasoning mix.

Heat a very large cast-iron skillet large enough to hold the chops in a single layer without crowding over medium-high heat until hot but not smoking, 3 1/2 to 4 minutes. Meanwhile, rub about 1 teaspoon of the seasoning mix into each side of the pork chops.

Once the skillet is hot, brush it with oil, and lay the chops in the pan with the thickest parts toward the center. Season with salt and cook for 3 minutes; turn, season the other side with salt, and cook for 2 1/2 to 3 minutes or until the meat measures 125° to 130°F on an instant-read thermometer inserted into the thickest part of one chop close to the bone. Immediately remove the chops to a cutting board, tent with aluminum foil, and let them rest for 5 minutes.

While the chops rest, warm the mushrooms and serve the chops with them spooned on top.

# Southern Seasoning Mix

1 tablespoon chili powder

½ tablespoon each ground coriander, cumin, garlic powder, salt, and
  ground black pepper

2 teaspoons firmly packed dark brown sugar

½ teaspoon cayenne

¼ teaspoon ground cinnamon

Combine the ingredients in a small bowl or jar and mix well.

# Polish Pork and Cabbage Stew *(Bigos)*

## *Serves 6*

1 ounce dried Polish or Italian porcini mushrooms

2 tablespoons canola or vegetable oil

5 ounces thick-sliced bacon, diced

1 pound lean boneless pork stew meat, cut into 1-inch cubes and patted dry

3 large yellow onions, peeled and coarsely chopped

1 small or ½ medium green cabbage, cored and shredded

3 cloves garlic, peeled and minced

2 cups beef stock

1 cup hearty red wine, such as cabernet sauvignon

2 cups canned tomatoes with juice, chopped

1 pound sauerkraut, rinsed under cold water and squeezed dry

1 cup pitted dried prunes, chopped

12 juniper berries, bruised

2 bay leaves

4 ounces cooked ham, diced

8 ounces kielbasa, casings removed and cut into ½-inch slices

Salt and freshly ground black pepper

Sour cream, to garnish

After I had endured a far-too-long and trying renovation of my dining room, our charming artisan-wood restorer Zaby brought me a peace offering of bigos. The formidable casserole is the national dish of Poland and is typically made with sauerkraut and fresh cabbage, a variety of pork products (including ham, kielbasa, and fresh pork), and either an apple or prunes to balance the tangy flavors.

Originally eaten by aristocrats, as they were the only people allowed to hunt game on their estates, there are many versions, including some with game, beef, and veal along with the slowly cooked pork and cabbage that make this dish so beloved. Serve it with boiled potatoes, sour cream, and rye or pumpernickel bread. It improves with reheating.

Soak the mushrooms in 1 cup warm water until softened, about 20 minutes. Drain the liquid through two layers of dampened paper towels into a container and reserve; remove any grit from the mushrooms and set aside.

Heat a 10-inch cast-iron Dutch oven over medium heat until just hot, about 3 minutes. Add the oil and bacon and cook until the fat is rendered from the bacon. With a slotted spoon, remove the bacon to a paper towel and reserve.

Raise the heat to medium-high, add the stew meat, and brown on all sides, 8 to 10 minutes; remove the pieces with a slotted spoon to a bowl. Turn the heat back down to medium, stir in the onions and cabbage, and cook until the onions are wilted and golden, 6 to 8 minutes, stirring often.

Add the garlic and cook for 30 seconds, then stir in the stock, reserved mushroom liquid, wine, tomatoes, sauerkraut, prunes, juniper berries, and bay leaves and bring to a boil, scraping up any browned bits on the bottom. Reduce the heat to low, cover, and simmer for 2 hours. Uncover, stir in the ham and kielbasa, and cook for 30 minutes longer; season to taste with salt and a liberal amount of black pepper. Remove the bay leaves, and serve the stew in wide soup bowls with a dollop of sour cream, if using, and a little bacon sprinkled on top. If desired, serve with boiled potatoes.

# Bratwursts and Sauerkraut

*Serves 4 to 6*

*The combination of sausages and sauerkraut has been a staple of Midwestern cooking ever since German settlers arrived there centuries ago. The tangy cured cabbage along with sautéed onions and beer are the perfect partner for grilled or sautéed brats. There are many delicious sausages available today that would work in this partnership. Serve them with coarse-grained mustard...and pitchers of ice-cold beer.*

2 tablespoons canola or vegetable oil + oil to sauté the bratwursts

5 ounces (about 1 cup) thick-sliced bacon, cut into ½-inch cubes

2 large yellow onions, peeled and sliced

12 ounces (1 ½ cups) lager or German-style beer

1 large sweet apple, such as an Empire or Gala, peeled, cored, and grated or finely chopped

10 juniper berries, bruised

2 bay leaves

1 tablespoon firmly packed light brown sugar

2 teaspoons caraway seeds

Salt and freshly ground black pepper

2 pounds sauerkraut, drained, rinsed and squeezed dry

12 bratwursts

Coarse-grained mustard

Heat a large, cast-iron Dutch oven or deep skillet over medium-high heat until hot, about 3 1/2 minutes. Add the oil and the bacon and cook until the bacon is crisp, about 5 minutes, turning often. Using a slotted spoon, remove the cubes, blot on paper towels, and set aside.

Stir in the onions, then reduce the heat to low, partially cover the pot, and cook until the onions are very tender and lightly browned, about 15 minutes, stirring occasionally. Pour in the beer, stirring up any browned cooking bits; then add the apple, juniper berries, bay leaves, brown sugar, caraway seeds, about 1 teaspoon of salt, or to taste, and a generous amount of black pepper. Stir in the sauerkraut, turn the heat to medium-high, and bring to a boil; then reduce the heat to low, cover, and cook until the apple is tender, 40 to 45 minutes, stirring occasionally.

Chop the reserved bacon into small pieces, stir it into the sauerkraut, and cook for 5 minutes longer. Remove and discard the bay leaves before serving.

About 10 minutes before the sauerkraut mixture has finished cooking, prick the sausages in several places with a fork. Heat a large skillet over medium-high heat, add enough oil to cover the bottom of the pan, and cook the sausages until lightly browned and heated through, 6 to 8 minutes, turning often. Serve the sauerkraut on a large platter with the sausages on top; accompany with mustard.

SEAFOOD

"The Secret of Good Cooking is: First, be a critical judge—known excellent cooking from poor cooking; Second, find a fascination in the science, and become thoroughly familiar with 'what, and what not to do'; Third, find a genuine pleasure in the practice—mastering the basic recipes and the operation and control of your Range—and above all, 'THINK.'"

*–Aunt Ellen*

# Panko-Macadamia-Crusted Salmon with Corn, Pepper, and Scallion Salsa

*Serves 4*

The crunchy macadamia-panko crust on these salmon fillets adds a surprisingly flavorful layer to the fish. It is complemented by the colorful corn, bell pepper, and scallion salsa. A little bit of orange juice concentrate makes all the flavors sparkle. Serve the fish either warm or at room temperature.

2 tablespoons mayonnaise

1 teaspoon paprika

1/2 cup macadamia nuts

1/2 cup panko bread crumbs, found in the Asian food section of supermarkets

2 teaspoons fresh thyme leaves or 1/2 teaspoon dried leaves

4 (6-ounce) boneless salmon fillets with skin on

Salt and freshly ground black pepper

Canola or vegetable oil to sauté the fish and cook the corn

Salsa (recipe follows)

Preheat your oven to 425°F.

In a small bowl, blend the mayonnaise and paprika. In a food processor, combine the macadamia nuts, panko, thyme leaves, and a generous pinch of salt, and process until fairly finely chopped.

Heat a 12-inch cast-iron skillet over medium heat until hot but not smoking, 3 1/2 to 4 minutes. Season the salmon lightly with salt and pepper. With the flesh side up, spread a thin layer of mayonnaise over each salmon fillet. Spoon about 2 tablespoons of the macadamia mixture onto the mayonnaise, pressing it gently into the flesh.

Pour enough oil into the skillet to measure 1/8-inch. Add the fillets, coated-side down, and cook until the crust is golden brown, about 2 1/2 minutes, using a thin metal spatula to lift and check. Do not turn. Transfer the pan to the oven and bake until the salmon is just cooked through, 7 to 8 minutes.

Meanwhile, make the salsa.

When the salmon is cooked, serve the fillets with the salsa spooned on top or as a bed underneath each piece.

. . . . . . . . . . . . . . . . . . . . . . . . . . . . . . . . . . . . .

## Salsa

1 ½ tablespoons canola or vegetable oil
1 cup fresh, defrosted frozen, or canned corn kernels, drained
½ cup finely chopped red bell pepper
2 large scallions, including most of the green parts, thinly sliced
1 to 2 tablespoons minced fresh jalapeño pepper
2 tablespoons orange juice concentrate
1 tablespoon minced fresh ginger root
2 teaspoons chopped fresh thyme leaves or ½ dried thyme leaves
1 ½ teaspoons honey
Salt and freshly ground black pepper

Heat 1/2 tablespoon of oil in a small skillet over high heat until hot. Add the corn and sauté until lightly colored, 1 to 2 minutes, shaking the pan often. Scrape the corn into a bowl along with the bell pepper, scallions, and jalapeño pepper.

In a 1-cup glass measuring cup, combine the orange juice concentrate, ginger, and thyme; heat in a microwave oven on high just until boiling, about 30 seconds. Remove, stir in the honey, and cool for 1 minute. Whisk in the remaining 1 tablespoon of oil, and toss with the corn salsa. Season with salt and pepper to taste.

# Southern Fried Catfish

*Serves 2*

*Cast-iron fried catfish is the epitome of Southern cooking. These fillets are super-crunchy and golden on the outside, yet tender inside thanks to a quick bath in buttermilk. You can cook other flat white fish this way, too. Serve the fillets with Glazed Butternut Squash (page 64) and sautéed greens, like collards or dandelions. This recipe may be doubled, in which case, turn your oven to warm before starting to fry the fish and cook them in two batches. Homemade Tartar Sauce is easily made while the fish is soaking.*

½ cup buttermilk

2 skinless catfish fillets, about ¾ pound

¼ cup yellow cornmeal

2 tablespoon unbleached all-purpose flour

½ tablespoon Southern Seasoning Mix (page 151)

Salt

Canola or grapeseed oil, for frying

Lemon wedges, to garnish

Homemade Tartar Sauce (recipe follows) or purchased tartar or remoulade sauce

Rinse the catfish fillets under cold water, pat dry, and put them in a resealable plastic bag with the buttermilk; seal and let them soak for 15 minutes. In a shallow bowl or plate, combine the cornmeal, flour, and Southern Seasoning Mix, stirring to blend evenly.

While the fish soak, make the Homemade Tartar Sauce, if using. Line a plate with paper towels.

Heat a 10-inch cast-iron skillet over medium-high heat until hot but not smoking, 3 1/2 to 4 minutes. Pour in enough oil to measure 1/4-inch deep. When a little cornmeal sprinkled on the oil foams, the oil is hot enough. It should not be smoking. If it is, turn off the heat and let the oil cool a little.

Lift each fillet from the buttermilk, letting the excess drip off. Dip the catfish in the cornmeal mixture, taking care to cover it completely, and patting to remove any excess. Season both sides with salt. Put the fillets in the hot oil and cook until golden brown, 2 1/2 to 3 minutes; turn and cook the other side for the same amount of time. Blot dry on paper towels and serve at once with lemon wedges and tartar sauce.

## Homemade Tartar Sauce
*Makes 1/2 cup*

⅓ cup mayonnaise

¼ cup minced dill pickles

3 tablespoons minced shallots

2 tablespoons minced cilantro leaves or flat-leaf parsley

2 teaspoons minced capers

1 teaspoon freshly squeezed lemon juice

Tabasco sauce to taste

Stir all of the ingredients together in a small bowl.

# Fillet of Sole with Browned Lemon-Caper Butter

*Serves 2*

*This is another quick and delicious way to cook fillet of sole or most any flat white fish. Vary the cooking times with the thickness of the fish. Sole takes the minimum time; tilapia takes about 15 to 30 seconds longer per side. Brussels Sprouts with Pistachios and Bacon (page 70), Oven-Roasted Asparagus with Macadamia Nuts (page 74), or sautéed green beans, along with cooked rice or couscous, are all fine side dishes to serve with the fish.*

2 large sole fillets, each 5 ½ to 6 ounces, rinsed and blotted dry

Salt and freshly ground black pepper

Unbleached all-purpose flour, for dredging

2 tablespoons unsalted butter, at room temperature

1 tablespoon freshly squeezed lemon juice

1 teaspoon small capers in brine

1 ½ teaspoons finely chopped flat-leaf parsley

Preheat your oven to 200°F. Put a plate in to warm.

Season the fillets with salt and pepper; dredge them in flour, patting to remove the excess.

Heat a 10-inch cast-iron skillet over high heat until hot but not smoking, 3 1/2 to 4 minutes. Add 1 tablespoon of the butter, swirl to cover the bottom of the pan, then immediately add the fillets and sauté for 2 to 2 1/2 minutes, depending on the thickness of the fish, until golden brown; turn and cook the other side until lightly browned and just cooked through, about 2 minutes. Transfer the fish to the plate to keep warm.

Add the remaining butter to the skillet and cook until light brown; stir in the lemon juice and capers, bring just to a boil, and turn off the heat. Stir in the parsley, and season to taste with salt and pepper. Spoon the lemon-caper butter over the fish and serve immediately.

*Fish served with a mixture of tomatoes, capers, olives, and onions is the most famous dish from the Mexican state of Veracruz. The capital city, also called Veracruz, is on the Gulf of Mexico. It has been a busy trade port for centuries. As a result, the food reflects influences from the Mediterranean to the Caribbean and, especially in this dish, Spain.*

*In Veracruz, red snapper or bass fillets are typically used in this dish, but any mild, meaty fillets will work. Some of my favorites are hake or grouper, depending on what I find in the market. While the sauce simmers, the fish is first seared over high heat on top of the stove and then baked in the oven. In Mexico, the dish is usually garnished with purchased pickled jalapeños and accompanied by boiled rice. It can also be served at room temperature, in which case, the tomato mixture can be made several hours ahead of time.*

Preheat your oven to 400°F.

In a large non-reactive skillet, heat the 2 tablespoons of olive oil over medium-high heat until hot. Add the onions, reduce the heat to medium, and sauté until translucent, about 4 minutes, stirring occasionally; add the garlic and cook for 30 seconds. Stir in the tomatoes, olives, capers, oregano, cinnamon, cloves, and bay leaves. Stir in the wine and bring to a boil, then reduce the heat and simmer for 15 minutes, stirring occasionally. Stir in the lime juice and salt and pepper to taste, and cook 30 seconds longer. Remove the bay leaves.

# Veracruz-Style Fish Fillets

*Serves 4*

2 tablespoons olive oil + 1 tablespoon oil to cook the fish

1 medium yellow onion, peeled and sliced crosswise

3 to 4 large cloves garlic, peeled and thinly sliced

1 (28-ounce) can high-quality diced tomatoes, drained (2 cups)

1/2 cup thinly sliced Spanish green olives with pimentos

1/4 cup small capers

1 1/2 tablespoons dried oregano, preferably Mexican

1 teaspoon ground cinnamon

3 to 4 whole cloves

2 bay leaves

1/4 cup dry white wine

2 to 3 teaspoons freshly squeezed lime juice

Salt and freshly ground black pepper

4 (6-ounce) firm white fish fillets, such as hake, haddock or tilapia, rinsed and blotted dry

Sliced pickled jalapeños, for garnish

Meanwhile, heat a cast-iron skillet large enough to comfortably hold the fish in a single layer without crowding over high heat until hot. Brush the skillet with the remaining oil. After seasoning the fish fillets on both sides with salt and pepper, lay them in the pan and brown them on both sides, about 3 minutes per side, carefully turning them with a metal spatula. Then transfer the skillet to the oven to bake until the fillets are done, 4 to 5 minutes, depending on the thickness of the fish. Garnish each fillet with a few sliced jalapeños, if desired, and spoon the sauce around the fish. Serve at once.

# Finnan Haddie

*Serves 6 generously*

Many people think of Finnan Haddie as a heavy, white sauce-laced casserole that is kind of boring. That certainly isn't the case with Pam Harding's tasty fish-and-potato combination made with smoked fish and bacon. It's perfect for a winter's night or as part of a cold-weather buffet. The dish, popular in New England, is said to have originated in Scotland—from the coastal town of Findhorn, or Findon—where smoked fish is usually eaten at breakfast. I love bacon in this dish (or almost anywhere), but if your smoked haddock, cod, trout, bluefish, or salmon has a very pronounced smoke flavor, you might omit it. In that case, use a little butter in the bottom of the pan.

6 slices bacon

3 pounds russet or other baking potatoes

4 tablespoons unbleached all-purpose flour

4 tablespoons unsalted butter, cut into small pieces

Salt and freshly ground black pepper

1 to 1 ¼ pounds smoked haddock or other fish (see above), skin and bones removed, chopped into small pieces

1 medium yellow onion, peeled and finely chopped

2 teaspoons finely chopped fresh thyme leaves or ½ teaspoon dried

3 cups whole milk or light cream

1 ¼ cup crushed oyster crackers

Preheat your oven to 350°F.

Put the bacon in a 10-inch cast-iron Dutch oven, turn the heat to medium, and cook until crisp. Remove the slices to paper towels, blot dry, and chop into small pieces. Discard all but about 1 teaspoon of fat in the bottom of the pan.

Meanwhile, peel and slice the potatoes about 1/8-inch thick (a food processor works well); put them in a bowl of cold water. Just before you are ready to use them, drain well and transfer the slices to a microwave-safe dish or bowl, cover with a paper towel, and cook in the microwave oven on high until the slices begin to soften, about 5 minutes. Layer a quarter of the potatoes in the bottom of the Dutch oven. Sprinkle on a tablespoon of flour, dot with a tablespoon of butter, and season with a scant 1/2 teaspoon each salt and freshly ground black pepper.

Scatter one third of the fish, onion, and thyme over the potatoes. Repeat twice more. Finish with the remaining potatoes. Pour the milk or cream down the side of the pan, sprinkle on the oyster crackers, and dot the top with butter. Bake until the top is golden brown and the potatoes are tender, about 1 hour. Remove and let stand for at least 10 minutes before serving.

## Cast-Iron Smoked Fish

*Pam Harding likes to smoke oily fish such as fresh-caught bluefish or salmon with the skin on. Make a rub of equal parts salt, sugar, and black pepper. Rub it on both sides of the raw fish and refrigerate for at least an hour. Remove the fish from the refrigerator and rub lightly with olive oil on both sides.*

*To prepare the pan: Line the bottom and sides of a deep skillet with aluminum foil. Tear about a 2-inch hole in the foil in the center of the pan and add about a tablespoon of real wood chips (alder or whatever you are using, so long as they are wood chips, not powder). Some people soak the chips first in water, but Pam usually doesn't bother.*

*Place a metal rack in the pan about an inch off the bottom. (You can also use strategically placed foil balls to elevate the rack.) Lay the fish skin-side down on the rack. Cover with an aluminum foil-lined cover and pinch the foil around the sides to seal it well so the smoke doesn't escape. (The foil also makes for easier cleanup.)*

*Put the pan over high heat. After about 15 minutes, peek inside to see if fish is done. Much will depend on the thickness of the fish. Pam uses fish that is about 3/4- to 1-inch thick. Smoking usually takes about 20 minutes. Sometimes the fish turns a lovely russet color, sometimes not.*

# Seared Swordfish over Ginger-Sesame Noodles with Asian Vinaigrette

*Serves 4*

¹⁄₃ cup hoisin sauce

¹⁄₄ cup rice vinegar

2 tablespoons soy sauce

1 tablespoon minced fresh ginger root

1 large clove garlic, peeled and minced

¹⁄₄ cup toasted sesame oil + 1 tablespoon oil to drizzle on the noodles

2 tablespoons canola oil

1 to 2 teaspoons hot chili pepper oil

6 ounces uncooked Japanese soba noodles

2 scallions, thinly sliced, including most of the green parts + thinly sliced scallions to garnish

1 small red bell pepper, seeds and membranes removed, and thinly sliced

1 cup steamed small broccoli florets

4 (1-inch thick) swordfish steaks, about 6 ounces each, blotted dry

Coarse ground black pepper

Coarse sea salt

2 tablespoons sesame seeds, lightly toasted

*Cast-iron skillets have long been used to cook traditional fare. They also shine when cooking fish that is seared on the outside and rare to medium-rare on the inside. These swordfish steaks coated with cracked pepper and sea salt need no oil in a very hot, well-seasoned pan, yet they are succulent and flavorful. Soba noodles tossed with the same vinaigrette used on the swordfish, make an eye-appealing room-temperature base on which to serve the fish.*

In a small bowl, blend the hoisin sauce, vinegar, soy sauce, ginger, and garlic together. Whisk in sesame and canola oils, add 1 teaspoon of the hot chili pepper oil, and set aside.

Preheat your oven to 400°F.

Meanwhile, cook the soba noodles as directed on the package; drain well and combine them in a large bowl with the scallions, bell pepper, and broccoli. Drizzle with the remaining 1 tablespoon of sesame oil and toss.

Heat a cast-iron skillet large enough to hold the swordfish steaks comfortably in a single layer over high heat until very hot but not smoking, 3 1/2 to 4 minutes. Press the cracked pepper into both sides of the swordfish, lay the steaks in the pan, season with salt, and cook for 3 minutes without moving them. Then turn the steaks, season the other side with salt, and cook 2 minutes more. Transfer the pan to the oven and cook until the fish is done to your taste, 2 to 4 minutes,

## Swordfish on the Grill Pan

*Many stylish restaurants serve thick swordfish steaks either cooked over a fiery charcoal grill or in a cast-iron grill pan. If you have a grill pan, heat it over high heat until very hot. Brush the steaks (marinated or plain) with a little oil and lay them in the pan. Cook them for half the time you would normally cook each side—say, 2 minutes for a 1 1/4-inch-thick steak—then brush with a little oil and turn them over to cook on the other side. Repeat grilling the steaks on both sides, rotating them about a quarter turn from where the original grill marks are to finish cooking and create those attractive cross-hatch grill marks.*

depending on the thickness of the fish. Remove and let stand while finishing the noodles.

Toss the noodles with 6 tablespoons of the vinaigrette, tasting to adjust the seasonings, and adding more chili oil, if desired; divide them among four dinner plates. Cut the swordfish across the grain into 1/2-inch slices, and lay these over the noodles. Drizzle on some of the remaining vinaigrette, garnish with the sesame seeds and a few scallions, and serve. Pass any remaining vinaigrette at table.

# GRISWOLD kitchen utensils live through many holiday seasons

*Griswold Tite-Top Dutch Oven*

*Griswold Cast Iron Skillet*

*Griswold Griddle*

*Griswold Heart-Star Gem Pan*

YOU'RE really building for the future when you select Griswold cast iron utensils for your kitchen. It's wonderful how, instead of wearing out, they become more useful and more thoroughly indispensable every year.

Griswold cast iron utensils endear themselves to their owners because they make it easy to cook tempting things to eat and because they need not be replaced.

That is why your friends are delighted to receive Griswold utensils for Christmas—if you look over your list carefully, you are sure to find several names at least for whom one of these articles will be just the most welcome and appropriate gift.

If your local dealer cannot supply you, we shall be glad to see that you get what you want.

## THE GRISWOLD MFG. CO.
Dept. R-2, Erie, Penna., U. S. A.

*Griswold Standard Waffle Iron (Also made in Heart-Star Design)*

*Makers of the Bolo Oven, Extra Finished Iron Kitchen Ware, Waffle Irons, Cast Aluminum Cooking Utensils, Food Choppers, Reversible Dampers and Gas Hot Plates.*

# Paella

*Serves 6*

3 cups chicken stock

¼ teaspoon saffron threads

2 tablespoons olive oil

1 large yellow onion, peeled and diced

4 skinless, boneless chicken thighs, cut into bite-size pieces and patted dry

¼ pound chorizo, casing removed and cut into ¼-inch slices

Salt and freshly ground black pepper

1 cup short-grained Spanish rice

½ pound large shrimp, peeled and deveined

½ pound squid, cleaned and cut crosswise into ½-inch rings

6 to 12 cherrystone clams, scrubbed

1 roasted red bell pepper, seeds and membranes removed, and diced

1 cup frozen peas, defrosted

½ cup small pitted green olives with pimento

¼ cup coarsely chopped flat-leaf parsley

*Paella is Spain's most famous dish. Although said to have originated in Valencia, there are numerous versions of this dish. Most often they are made with seafood, chicken, and rice. During the years I lived in Paris, and before I had been to Spain, some very close friends had a Portuguese cook named Maria. The wonderful aroma that wafted through the house when she was cooking this fragrant stew never failed to draw me to the kitchen. While my version has changed over the years, memories of this sunny dish, my years in Paris, and subsequent visits to Spain endure.*

Heat 2 1/2 cups of the chicken stock and saffron in a small pan or in the microwave until boiling. Set aside.

Heat a 10-inch cast-iron Dutch oven or deep skillet over medium-high heat until hot but not smoking, 3 1/2 to 4 minutes. Add the oil and onion and cook until golden, 3 to 4 minutes. Add the chicken and brown on all sides, about 4 minutes, turning often. Stir in the chorizo and cook for 2 minutes. Add the rice, stirring to coat with the oil, and cook for about 2 minutes, shaking to distribute the grains evenly in the bottom of the pan.

Slowly pour enough stock into the pot or pan to cover the ingredients. Add the shrimp, squid, and clams; cover, reduce the heat to low, and simmer until the rice is almost tender, about 25 minutes, adding more stock if needed. Remove the lid, stir in the bell pepper, peas, and olives. Once the rice is cooked, stir in the parsley and remove the pot from the heat. Cover with a dish towel and let the paella rest for 5 minutes before giving the pot a few stirs. Discard any clams that do not open before serving.

# Jambalaya—Paella's First Cousin

## *Serves 6 to 8*

1 ½ pounds bone-in chicken thighs and breasts or 2 rotisserie chickens

1 tablespoon canola or vegetable oil

1 cup chopped yellow onion

¾ cup sliced celery

½ each: medium red + green bell peppers, seeds and membranes removed, and diced

8 ounces sliced andouille or smoked ham

2 large cloves garlic, peeled and finely chopped

1 ½ cups uncooked long-grained rice

2 ½ to 3 cups chicken broth

1 cup canned plum tomatoes with juice, coarsely chopped

1 cup purchased tomato basil pasta sauce

2 pounds large shrimp, peeled and deveined

1 tablespoon Worcestershire sauce

½ to 1 tablespoon lemon juice (optional)

1 teaspoon sugar (optional)

1 tablespoon chopped flat-leaf parsley

1 teaspoon Creole seasoning or ¼ teaspoon cayenne or Tabasco sauce (see note)

½ teaspoon dried thyme leaves

Salt and freshly ground black pepper

Chopped scallions, including green parts, to garnish

*Paella and jambalaya have a lot in common: both are simmered together in a single pot with rice, vegetables, sausage, chicken or meat, seafood, and stock. While saffron imparts the characteristic yellow color to the Spanish dish, tomatoes give the Creole version its red tone. The Cajun version typically includes browned meat without tomatoes.*

*Anne Semmes is a Baton Rouge native. Her version of jambalaya combines the "usual suspects": chicken, shrimp, andouille sausage, bell peppers, and rice with traditional seasonings into a most agreeable one-dish meal. Anne says jambalaya is such a good make-ahead party dish because you can prepare it several hours ahead, up to the addition of the shrimp, and then finish it once your guests arrive. The flavors will improve as it sits. It can also be doubled to serve a crowd. While the ingredient list is long, jambalaya takes very little work and is well worth the effort.*

If using uncooked chicken parts, remove the skin and poach them in simmering water seasoned with salt and pepper until just done. Cool, remove the bones, and cut the chicken into large chunks; reserve in the refrigerator. Or skin and bone the rotisserie chickens and cut into chunks.

Heat a 10-inch cast-iron Dutch oven over medium heat until hot, about 3 minutes; add the oil, onions, and celery, partially cover, and sweat the vegetables over low heat until limp, 5 to 7 minutes. Stir in the bell peppers, sausage or ham, and garlic and sauté for 2 to 3 minutes. Add the rice, the smaller amount

**178**

of the chicken broth, plum tomatoes, and pasta sauce. Turn
the heat to high and bring to boil, then stir, cover tightly,
reduce the heat, and simmer for 20 minutes without removing
the lid.

Remove the lid and put the chicken and shrimp on top of the
rice. Re-cover the pot and simmer until the shrimp are cooked
through, 3 to 4 minutes. Add the Worcestershire, lemon juice
and/or sugar (if using), parsley, Creole seasoning or cayenne,
and thyme leaves; season to taste with salt and pepper. Add the
remaining chicken broth if needed. If there seems to be too
much liquid, gently boil it a little longer. It should be soupy.

*Note:* Anne Semmes says that Tony Chachere's Seasoning's
can be purchased online. She adds that both Emeril Lagasse
and Paul Prudhomme sell similar seasonings, so the best
advice is "season to taste."

# Shrimp Posole

*Serves 4*

*Native Americans have given us many culinary gifts including clambakes from tribes in New England, and this soupy stew, known as posole (or pozole), from tribes who roamed the Southwest before Christopher Columbus arrived. Hominy is the dried kernel of corn with the hull and germ removed. Pam Harding has served this satisfying main dish for years. It can also be made with pork and chicken, in which case you would brown the cubes of meat first.*

1 pound tomatillos, husked

2 chipotles chiles in adobo

2 tablespoons olive oil

1 medium yellow onion, peeled and finely chopped

3 to 4 large garlic cloves, peeled and finely chopped

1 teaspoon each ground cumin and ground coriander

3 to 4 cups chicken stock

1 (28-ounce) can hominy, preferably white, drained and rinsed

1 cup defrosted frozen or canned corn kernels, drained

1 teaspoon oregano, preferably Mexican

Salt and freshly ground black pepper

1 pound peeled and deveined large shrimp

1/4 cup chopped cilantro leaves

Bring a medium-sized pot of water to a boil, add the tomatillos, and gently boil until soft, about 8 minutes. Drain the tomatillos, add them to the jar of an electric blender with the chipotles, and purée.

Meanwhile, heat a 10-inch cast-iron Dutch oven over medium-high heat until hot but not smoking, 3 1/2 to 4 minutes. Add the oil, onions, and garlic and sauté until the onion is soft, 3 to 4 minutes. Sprinkle the cumin and coriander into the pan and stir until fragrant, about 1 minute. Add the tomatillo-chipotle mixture, 3 cups of the stock, the hominy, corn, and oregano; cover and simmer for 30 minutes. Remove the lid, season with about 1 teaspoon of salt and plenty of freshly ground black pepper, and cook 10 minutes longer. Add the shrimp, cover, and cook until done, 3 to 4 minutes. For a soupier texture, pour in as much of the remaining stock as you wish and heat until hot. Stir in the cilantro and serve in shallow soup bowls.

# Aunt Ellen's Delicious Kitchen Tested Dishes

## COD-FISH CAKES

Prepare about 3 pounds salt cod for cooking; after draining, pick out any bones, and add about 5 medium, well-washed, thinly sliced potatoes and 1/2 cup cold water. Cook over moderate heat about 20 minutes, then add 1 tablespoon butter. Remove from fire, season with a little white pepper; and, with a potato-masher, mash all together in the pan. Transfer to a dish and cool. Make into cakes or balls, dust well with a little flour, and drop into hot deep frying fat. Fry to a nice brown color, lift out with a skimmer very gently, and serve on folded napkin on hot plate. Garnish with parsley.

## OYSTER STEW

Put 1 quart fresh oysters in a strainer placed over a stew pan. Pour over the oysters 3/4 cup cold water, letting it run into the liquor. Carefully pick over the oysters, removing any bits of shell. Heat liquor to boiling point and skim thoroughly. Add 4 cups of milk and 1 cup cream, and when it boils, add 1 tablespoon each flour and butter rubbed together, and mix to smoothness; season with salt and pepper to taste. Keep hot until ready to serve. Now, just before carrying to table, bring liquid to boiling point, remove from over fire to prevent further boiling, and pour in the oysters. When they have cooked enough to be plump and the edges begin to curl, serve. If all milk and no cream has been used, double the amount of butter. Never allow milk to reach a boil after putting in the oysters, as they will be toughened, and the quality of the stew spoiled. Serve with oyster crackers.

# Crawfish and Shrimp Étouffée

*Serves at least 12*

*Anne Semmes's version of crawfish and shrimp étouffée, the famed Creole stew, is robust and seductive. One bite quickly leads to the next. Anne starts her stew with a roux—flour and oil slowly cooked and stirred until the mixture turns a golden nut brown—to thicken the sauce and deepen the flavor. She also includes tomatoes. While both additions are debated among locals, I'm sure you will find this version to be sensational.*

¼ cup canola or vegetable oil

¼ cup unbleached all-purpose flour

1 cup chopped yellow onion

¾ cup sliced celery

1 bell pepper (any color), seeds and membranes removed, and chopped

2 large cloves garlic, peeled and minced

2 ½ to 3 cups stock, preferably half chicken, half seafood), heated to a boil

½ cup tomato purée

1 teaspoon salt

½ teaspoon cayenne

¼ teaspoon freshly ground black pepper

3 tablespoons unsalted butter

1 pound crawfish tails

¾ pound large shrimp, peeled and deveined

¾ cup finely chopped scallions, including most of the green parts

¼ cup chopped flat-leaf parsley

6 to 8 cups cooked rice, heated

Heat the oil in a large cast-iron skillet over medium-high heat for 2 minutes. With a long-handled whisk, gradually mix in the flour, stirring until smooth. Continue cooking and whisking until the roux is the color of peanut butter, about 2 minutes. Remove the pot from the heat and immediately stir in the onion, celery, bell peppers, and garlic. Add the salt and half the amounts of the cayenne and black pepper, adding more to taste, and stirring with a wooden spoon until the mixture has cooled.

Gradually whisk in 2 cups of the boiling stock and the tomato purée; reduce the heat to low and simmer for 2 minutes, then set aside. The recipe can be made several hours ahead of time up to this point.

Before serving, melt the butter in a large cast-iron Dutch oven over medium heat. Add the crawfish and cook, stirring, for 1 minute. Add the shrimp and vegetable-roux mixture and cook, shaking the pan back and forth without stirring it, for 5 minutes or until the crawfish are tender. Add more stock, as needed, so the consistency is like a soupy stew. Stir in the scallions and half of the parsley; and taste to adjust the seasonings. Cook for 1 minute longer and serve.

On a serving platter or individual plates, mound the hot rice, sprinkle on the remaining parsley, and surround with the seafood mixture.

{ *Desserts* }

*I don't like blueberries, which, I know, for many summer fruit lovers is a sin. On the other hand, I adore raspberries and blackberries, so when I make the proverbial summer fruit crisp—that generations of bakers have made in cast-iron skillets—they are the berries I choose. I think you'll find the combination is fabulous!*

# Raspberry-Blackberry Crisp

*Serves 4 to 6*

Preheat your oven to 375°F. Put a baking sheet in the middle of the oven. Lightly butter a 10-inch cast-iron skillet.

In a large bowl, stir the cornstarch and lemon juice together until blended; add the berries and sugar, and gently stir to combine them evenly. Scrape the mixture into the skillet.

In the same bowl, combine the oatmeal, flour, brown sugar, salt, and butter. Using a fork or your fingers, stir the mixture until it is crumbly and blended, and scatter it over the berries. Transfer the skillet to the baking sheet in the oven and bake until the topping is set and the berries are bubbling, about 40 minutes. Remove and cool for at least 15 minutes before serving the crisp from the skillet with vanilla ice cream or whipped cream on top.

Unsalted butter to grease the skillet

1 tablespoon + 1 teaspoon cornstarch

1 tablespoon freshly squeezed lemon juice

4 cups mixed fresh blackberries and raspberries

1/2 to 2/3 cup sugar, depending on how sweet the berries are

2/3 cup quick-cooking oatmeal

1/3 cup unbleached all-purpose flour

1/3 cup firmly packed dark brown sugar

1/8 teaspoon salt

4 tablespoons unsalted butter, at room temperature

Vanilla ice cream or sweetened whipped cream

# Plum Clafoutis

*Serves 6*

*Clafoutis is a classic French dessert—a puffy, custardy, fruit-filled pancake. Most often they are made with cherries, but my favorite fruit for this dish is plums. Serve it warm, straight from the pan either for brunch or dessert. Pfannkuchen (page 196) is another puffy pancake made with apples.*

½ cup unbleached all-purpose flour

½ cup + 3 tablespoons sugar

Pinch of salt

1 cup whole milk

3 large eggs

1 teaspoon almond extract

2 tablespoons unsalted butter

3 firm, ripe black plums (about 12 ounces), pitted and cut into medium slices

1 tablespoon plum brandy or cognac

Confectioners' sugar

Sweetened whipped cream or crème fraîche, to garnish

Preheat your oven to 425°F.

In a large bowl, sift the flour, the 1/2 cup of sugar, and salt. In a small bowl, blend the milk, eggs, and almond extract together, and then whisk them into the dry ingredients until smooth.

Heat the butter in a 10-inch cast-iron skillet over medium heat until melted and bubbling. Stir in the plums and cook them for 2 minutes, or until almost soft, turning occasionally. Sprinkle on the remaining 3 tablespoons of sugar, cook until the sugar is melted, then pour in the brandy or cognac and bring to a boil, shaking the pan to spread the fruit evenly.

Turn off the heat, pour the batter over the plums, and transfer the skillet to the oven. Bake until the clafouti is puffy, the edges are richly browned, and a knife inserted in the center comes out clean, about 18 minutes. Remove and let the clafoutis stand for 10 minutes, then sprinkle on some confectioners' sugar, and serve with a dollop of whipped cream or crème fraîche.

*Cobblers are among the most popular of Southern desserts. In this simple yet personal version, a ginger-spice batter is poured into the pan and topped by delicately rum-scented peaches. As it bakes, the crust rises to the top and almost covers the fruit. Serve the dessert directly from the skillet with ice cream or whipped cream.*

# Ginger-Spice-Topped Peach Cobbler

*Serves 8*

Preheat your oven to 350°F. Put a baking sheet in the middle of the oven.

In a large bowl, stir the rum and cornstarch until smooth. Add the peaches, sugar, and lemon juice and stir. Set aside.

In a 10-inch cast-iron skillet, heat the butter over medium heat until melted. Meanwhile, in a medium bowl, mix the flour, white and brown sugars, ginger, cinnamon, salt, and cloves. Whisk the milk and melted butter into the dry ingredients, leaving a thin coating of the butter on the bottom of the skillet.

Reheat the skillet over medium heat; pour in the batter and then add the peaches. Put the skillet on the baking sheet and bake until the cobbler's top is golden brown and the filling is bubbling, about 45 minutes. Remove from the oven and cool for at least 15 minutes, then serve the cobbler with vanilla ice cream or whipped cream.

**FILLING:**

3 tablespoons dark rum

2 ½ tablespoons cornstarch

2 (16-ounce) packages frozen peaches, defrosted

1 cup sugar

2 tablespoons freshly squeezed lemon juice

**TOPPING:**

6 tablespoons unsalted butter
   1 cup self-rising flour

⅓ cup sugar

⅓ cup firmly packed light brown sugar

1 teaspoon ground ginger

½ teaspoon cinnamon

¼ teaspoon salt

⅛ teaspoon ground clove

1 cup whole milk

Vanilla ice cream or sweetened whipped cream, to garnish

# Apple-Cherry Tarte Tatin

*Serves 8*

*This famous upside-down tart of caramelized apples and puff pastry was first made by the two Tatin sisters from France's Loire Valley. There are countless versions, including this one in which the thick apple slices are complemented by tangy dried cherries. When I can find Jonagold apples, I use them because they are sweet and juicy with just a touch of tartness. They also hold together while baking.*

¼ cup dried cherries

2 tablespoons apple brandy or Calvados

1 (15-ounce) package all-butter puff pastry, defrosted according to package directions

5 to 6 medium firm, tart-sweet apples, such as Jonagold, Cortland, Northern Spy, Golden Delicious

Juice of 1 to 2 lemons

¾ cup sugar

1 tablespoon water

4 tablespoons unsalted butter, cut into small pieces

Crème fraîche or sweetened whipped cream, to garnish

In a small bowl, combine the cherries with the brandy and set aside. Roll out the puff pastry on a lightly floured surface to a thickness of 1/8 inch. With a sharp knife, cut it into an 11-inch circle and brush off any excess flour. Lay the pastry on a cutting board, cover with a towel, and refrigerate.

Peel and core the apples; slice them in half lengthwise, then cut each half in thirds lengthwise. Put them in a large bowl and drizzle with lemon juice as you cut them to prevent discoloring.

Preheat your oven to 400°F.

Put the sugar in a 10-inch cast-iron skillet and drizzle on the water. Turn the heat to high and cook until the sugar melts into a rich, golden amber-colored syrup, 6 to 7 minutes, swirling and shaking the pan often to melt it evenly. Watch that it doesn't burn. Immediately remove the pan from the heat, add the butter (it might bubble up), and stir until it is incorporated. Continue stirring the mixture until the caramel

cools, 3 to 4 minutes. If the sugar seizes up when you add the butter, return the pan to the heat to re-melt it.

Lay the apple slices on the caramel around the outside of the pan, on their side and each in the same direction with the stem end closest to the pan's edge. Put the remaining apple slices in the center. (You may not need all of the apples.) Drain the cherries and add them around the edges, between each apple slice, and in the middle.

Remove the puff pastry from the refrigerator and lay it over the apples, pushing the edges down the sides of the pan. Cut 3 or 4 small gashes in the surface of the pastry as air vents, then transfer the skillet to the oven and bake for 10 minutes. Reduce the heat to 375° and bake for 20 minutes longer, or until the crust is golden brown and the syrup is bubbling up the sides.

Remove and cool the tart for about 20 minutes in the pan. Using a plate with a lip that is slightly larger than the skillet, put it upside down over the skillet and, holding them together with one hand, invert the skillet and let the tart slide out onto the plate, rearranging any apples that may have moved. Using a pie server with a sharp edge, cut the tart into slices and serve with a generous dollop of crème fraîche or whipped cream. You can also leave the tart in the pan and reheat it for 15 minutes in a preheated 375° oven.

# German-Style Apple Pancake

## (Pfannkuchen)

*Serves 4*

*I remember making this German-style apple pancake for my kids as they were growing up. They were always wide-eyed with excitement as I took the puffy pancake from the oven and added the confectioners' sugar and lemon juice that were the final garnishes before we cut it up and devoured it. Don't worry if the pancake collapses. It'll still be delectable.*

1 large tart-sweet apple, such as Cortland, peeled, cored, and thinly sliced

Juice and grated zest of 1 large lemon

4 large eggs, separated

½ cup whole milk

2 tablespoons sugar

2 tablespoons cornstarch

½ teaspoon salt

2 tablespoons unsalted butter

Confectioners' sugar, to garnish

Preheat your oven to 400°F. Position the rack in the middle of the oven. Heat a 10-inch cast-iron skillet over medium heat until hot, about 3 minutes.

In a bowl, combine the apple slices with 1 tablespoon of the lemon juice and set aside. In a large bowl, beat together the egg yolks, milk, sugar, cornstarch, salt, and lemon zest. In a separate large bowl, whisk the egg whites into soft peaks. Using a flexible spatula, gently fold the yolks into the whites until just mixed.

Add the butter to the heated skillet. When the butter foams, add the apples, turning to coat them with butter, and then arrange them in a single layer. Pour the egg mixture evenly over the apples. Partially cover, and cook for 10 minutes. Uncover the skillet, transfer it to the oven, and bake for about 15 minutes, or until the bottom of the *pfannkuchen* is nicely browned and it is set in the middle.

Remove, sprinkle with the confectioners' sugar and remaining lemon juice, and serve immediately.

# Tuscan Pineapple Upside-Down Cake

*Serves 8*

*Some years ago while visiting my friend, food writer Nancy Harmon Jenkins, in Tuscany, we had lunch with her neighbor, Mita Antolini, a local farmer. Mita made her "special dessert" in an old wood-burning stove. To my surprise, it turned out to be the best pineapple upside-down cake I'd ever tasted. The cake's texture was unique: kind of firm but light at the same time. I tried to re-create the effect of Italian durum wheat flour by adding a little whole-wheat flour to the batter. It is not especially sweet, so I serve it with sweetened whipped cream or vanilla ice cream.*

¾ cup sugar + ½ cup sugar

3 large eggs, separated

Grated zest of 1 lemon

1 (20-ounce) can sliced pineapple packed in its own juice, drained, juice reserved

2 tablespoons brandy or dark rum

1 teaspoon vanilla extract

1 ¼ cups unbleached all-purpose flour

½ cup whole wheat flour

1 ½ teaspoons baking soda

½ teaspoon salt

8 tablespoons (1 stick) unsalted butter, melted

1 cup chopped pecans or walnuts

Whipped cream or vanilla ice cream, to garnish

Preheat your oven to 350°F. Position a rack in the top third of the oven.

In a large bowl, beat together 3/4 cup sugar, the egg yolks, lemon zest, 1/2 cup of the reserved pineapple juice, the brandy, and vanilla until blended. Sift in the flours, baking soda, and salt; mix until smooth. Stir in the melted butter.

Heat the remaining 1/2 cup of sugar in a 10-inch cast-iron skillet over medium-high heat until the sugar melts and lightly caramelizes, about 5 minutes, rotating the pan often. Immediately remove the pan from the heat and continue to rotate to cool slightly. (The few remaining sugar crystals will melt in the residual heat while you are rotating the pan, so be careful not to over-brown the sugar while cooking.) Lay enough pineapple slices in the bottom of the skillet to cover (usually 7 or 8 slices), and sprinkle on the chopped nuts.

Beat the egg whites into soft peaks. Mix about a quarter of the whites into the batter; then fold in the remaining whites until blended. Spoon the batter evenly over the pineapple, taking care not to disturb the nuts, and spread with a metal spatula.

Bake in the top third of the oven until the cake is lightly browned on top and the center springs back when gently pressed with a finger, 25 to 27 minutes. Remove the skillet from the oven, run a knife around the inside edges, and carefully invert the cake onto a plate. Cool on a rack, cut into slices, and serve with whipped cream or ice cream.

*This dessert is decadence personified: luscious pecan-chocolate chunk cookies topped with great ice cream, and a "to die for" salted caramel sauce. The cookies are baked and served in individual cast-iron skillets. Although the recipe serves 12, bake as many cookies as you have guests and pans, and keep the remaining cookie dough and sauce in the refrigerator in covered containers. Or, freeze individual balls of dough and bake them whenever you want a special dessert. To serve 12, you could also bake one large cookie in a 10-inch cast-iron skillet and bring it to the table while still warm.*

# Chocolate Chunk–Pecan Cookie Sundaes with Salted Caramel Sauce

*Serves 12*

Preheat your oven to 350°F. Grease as many 6-inch cast-iron skillets as you will use or a 10-inch skillet with butter.

In a large bowl, cream the butter and sugars until smooth. Stir in the egg and vanilla. In another bowl, combine the flour, baking soda, and salt. Add the dry ingredients to the butter mixture and stir until smooth. Mix in the chocolate chunks and the pecans.

For each cookie, scoop out a level 1/4-cup measure of the dough (or weigh out 2-ounce portions on a kitchen scale) and put the dough in the center of the 6-inch pan. Repeat until all the pans are filled, then put them in the oven and bake until the cookies are lightly browned, about 13 to 15 minutes. Remove the pans and let them cool until the cookies are warm, not hot.

(Alternatively, put the dough into the 10-inch skillet, flatten into a 1-inch thick disc, and bake at 325° until done.)

1 stick (8 tablespoons) unsalted butter, at room temperature, + butter to grease pans

1/2 cup firmly packed dark brown sugar

1/2 cup sugar

1 large egg

1 teaspoon pure vanilla extract

1 cup + 2 tablespoons unbleached all-purpose flour

1/2 teaspoon baking soda

1/4 teaspoon salt

1 cup coarsely chopped dark chocolate chunks (about 6 ounces)

1/2 cup coarsely chopped pecans

Salted Caramel Sauce (recipe follows)

Vanilla or chocolate ice cream

Place a scoop of ice cream on each cookie (or cut the large cookie into 8 to 12 slices while still warm), drizzle on the caramel sauce, and serve.

. . . . . . . . . . . . . . . . . . . . . . . . . . . . . . . . . . . . . . . . .

## Salted Caramel Sauce
### *Makes about 2 cups*

1 ¼ cups sugar

⅓ cup water

3 tablespoons light corn syrup

1 cup heavy cream

5 tablespoons unsalted butter, at room temperature

1 ½ teaspoons coarse sea salt, finely crushed

In a medium saucepan, combine the sugar, water, and corn syrup and bring to a boil over high heat. Cook until the syrup turns a rich amber color, about 6 minutes, swirling the pan and washing down any crystals on the sides of the pan with a wet pastry brush to prevent them from burning. Remove the pan from the heat and whisk in the cream (it will bubble up, so be careful), butter, and salt. Set the sauce aside and serve warm.

# *Aunt Ellen's* Delicious Kitchen Tested Dishes

## CONFECTION WAFFLES

For tender, delicate Confection Waffles, use one cupful of rice boiled to a mush, and rubbed through a sieve; add two well-beaten egg yolks, two tablespoonfuls of sugar, one-half teaspoonful of salt—and beat until velvety. Measure out one cupful of flour sifted once with two teaspoonfuls of baking powder, and measure out a cup and a half of rich milk and melt one tablespoonful of butter. Add the flour and the milk alternately to the egg and rice mixture, beating hard; whip in half a cupful of finely chopped nut meats; then fold in the stiffly beaten whites of the two eggs, and the melted butter. Cook on hot Waffle Baker, and serve with hard sauce.

## FRENCH MELANGE

Ever eat a bouquet of flowers? French Melange is like that, really! Use two cupfuls of chopped rhubarb (tender stalks that have been put through the coarse blade or your Food Chopper without peeling them). Use two cupfuls of pineapple also chopped, and one cupful of fresh strawberries cut in quarters. Cover with four cupfuls of granulated sugar and let stand for an hour. Then put over the fire in the clean dry Skillet, stir once or twice; cover the Skillet, and let cook slowly over low heat for half an hour. By this time the Melange should begin to thicken. Add a half cupful of shredded almonds or walnuts and tablespoonful of grated orange rind. Leave uncovered and let cook till thick and clear. Stir very little during entire cooking process—distinct bits of fruit should show all through. Pour into glasses dipped in hot water and let cool before covering with paraffin. Serve on nut-buttered bread at tea.

# Chocolate Omelet Soufflé

## Serves 4

¼ cup coarsely chopped walnut pieces

1 teaspoon vanilla

8 ounces semisweet chocolate, melted

4 large eggs

⅓ cup heavy cream

3 tablespoons clarified butter

3 tablespoons confectioners' sugar

Sweetened whipped cream, to garnish

*If you are a chocoholic who loves simple yet intensely rich indulgences, Joe DiMaggio's dessert is a real treat and easy to make.*

Preheat your oven to 425°F.

Toss the walnuts with the vanilla. Scatter them on a baking sheet lined with aluminum foil and bake in the oven for 5 to 6 minutes, watching that they don't burn.

In a bowl, beat the eggs and cream to blend; add the melted chocolate and beat vigorously until frothy.

Heat a 10-inch cast iron skillet over medium heat until just hot, about 3 minutes; add the butter and walnuts, and cook for 30 seconds. Pour in the egg-chocolate mixture and cook for 1 minute. Transfer the skillet to the oven and bake until slightly firm, 8 to 9 minutes. Remove from the oven, and immediately invert the omelet onto a 10-inch plate. Dust with confectioners' sugar and cut in wedges, serving each portion with a generous dollop of whipped cream.

{ *Appendix* }

*One of the easiest ways to collect fixings for vegetable stock is to get in the habit of keeping vegetable trimmings including onion skins; carrot, turnip and potato peelings; and those wonderful dark green tops of leeks and celery hearts. Lots of chefs use papery onion skins in their stocks since they add color. The trick is to keep all the fixings in good condition. Unless you gather them within a day or two, it's best to freeze them in a resealable plastic bag, with all the air squeezed out, until you have a sizeable quantity. My vegetable stock differs each time I make it. What follows is a general plan. Don't forget lots of onions and garlic.*

Preheat your oven to 375° F. Brush a large, flat roasting pan with a little oil.

Scatter the chopped vegetables in the pan, turning to coat them evenly, and roast until they are a rich dark golden brown, turning often, 40 to 55 minutes depending on the size. Be sure they don't burn. Remove the pan from the oven and transfer the vegetables to a deep pot. Add the 2 quarts of water, parsley, thyme, and bay leaf, and bring to a boil.

Meanwhile, stir the warm water into the roasting pan, scraping up the browned cooking bits with a wooden spoon, and add it to the pot. Cover and simmer until the vegetables are very soft, 1 to 1 1/2 hours, and then strain through cheesecloth into a clean pot. Season to taste with salt and pepper. Cool and refrigerate until needed. It will keep for 3 to 4 days in the refrigerator. Or freeze for up to 3 months in airtight containers.

# VEGETABLE STOCK
## *Makes about 2 quarts*

1 tablespoon canola or other vegetable oil

5 large carrots, peeled and coarsely chopped

3 large unpeeled yellow onions, coarsely chopped

3 large stalks celery including leaves, coarsely chopped

2 large leeks, trimmed, rinsed, and split in half lengthwise

2 large cloves garlic, split

Leftover bell peppers, turnips, tomatoes, etc., chopped

2 quarts water

1/2 cup warm water

4 large sprigs flat-leaf parsley

3 sprigs fresh thyme

1 bay leaf

Salt and black pepper

# CHICKEN STOCK

*Makes about 4 quarts*

*This makes a lot of chicken stock, so you may want to cut the recipe in half. But if you use chicken stock as often as I do, it's just as easy to make a large quantity as a small amount, and then freeze it for future use.*

10 pounds chicken carcasses or wings, backs, and ribs, chopped into 1 ½-inch pieces (see Note)

3 large carrots, peeled and coarsely chopped

3 large unpeeled yellow onions, quartered

2 large stalks celery including leaves, coarsely chopped

6 large sprigs flat-leaf parsley

10 black peppercorns

3 bay leaves

1 tablespoon salt

1 ½ gallons water

Combine the chicken, carrots, onions, celery, parsley, peppercorns, bay leaves, and salt in a large deep stockpot. Add enough water to cover the chicken, about 1 1/2 gallons. Bring the water to just below the boiling point over high heat. Reduce the heat so the liquid is gently simmering, partially cover and cook for 2 to 2 1/2 hours, skimming off any scum that rises to the surface, then let cool.

When cool, strain the stock through cheesecloth. Do not press on the solids or the stock will become cloudy. Discard the bones, herbs, and vegetables. Cover and refrigerate for up to 3 days, or freeze for 5 to 6 months. Skim off the congealed surface fat before using.

*Note:* Get in the habit of saving chicken parts, such as the wings, backs and ribs, each time you cut up a chicken. Some markets sell these at a nominal cost. Put them into a resealable plastic bag or container and store in the freezer until you have a sufficient amount to make stock.

*This is a more robust tasting chicken stock than the previous version. It will last for 3 to 4 days in the refrigerator or for 6 months in the freezer.*

# RICH BROWN CHICKEN STOCK
*Makes 2 quarts*

Put the bones in a large deep skillet and cook over medium-high heat until golden brown, turning occasionally. Add the celery, carrot, onion, and garlic, and cook until the vegetables are golden brown, 7 to 8 minutes.

Stir in the tomato and tomato paste, cook for 5 minutes, then pour in the white wine and cook for 2 minutes more. Add the water, bay leaves, parsley, and thyme. Simmer for 1 hour, skimming the surface from time to time. Pour the liquid through a fine strainer into a clean pot. Season to taste with salt and pepper. If needed, reduce over high heat to the desired taste and consistency.

3 pounds chicken carcasses, wings, backs, and ribs, chopped into 1 ½-inch pieces

2 medium stalks celery including leaves, chopped

1 medium carrot, scraped and chopped

1 medium unpeeled yellow onion, coarsely chopped

5 garlic cloves, peeled and split in half

1 tomato, chopped

1 tablespoon tomato paste

½ cup dry white wine

2 quarts water

2 bay leaves

5 sprigs flat-leaf parsley

4 sprigs fresh thyme or 2 teaspoons dried thyme leaves

Salt and pepper

# MEAT STOCK
*Makes about 3 quarts*

*This flavorful beef stock is the basis for wonderful soups, stews, and sauces. Stock keeps for 3 days in the refrigerator or for 5 to 6 months when frozen.*

2 ½ pounds beef bones with some meat (shin, marrow, ribs), cracked if large

1 ½ pounds meaty veal shanks or knuckles, cracked if large

3 medium carrots, peeled and cut in 2-inch lengths

2 large unpeeled onions, split with 1 clove stuck in each half

1 leeks or the green tops of 2 leeks, trimmed, rinsed, and split in half lengthwise

1 large stalk celery including leaves, cut in 2-inch lengths

4+ quarts cold water

½ cup warm water

3 sprigs flat-leaf parsley

2 sprigs fresh thyme or 1 teaspoon dried

1 large clove garlic, peeled and split

5 black peppercorns

½ teaspoon salt, optional

Preheat your oven to 400° F.

Put the beef and veal bones in a large, shallow roasting pan and roast until browned on all sides, turning occasionally, 45 minutes to 1 hour. Pour off almost all the fat. Add the carrots, onions, cut-side down, leek, and celery to the pan and roast until the vegetables have started to brown and caramelize, about 15 minutes longer. Transfer the bones and vegetables to a large stockpot, add the cold water, and bring just to a boil. Adjust the heat down so the liquid is simmering. Skim off any scum that rises to the surface during the first hour.

Meanwhile, deglaze the roasting pan with the warm water, scraping up all the browned cooking bits with a wooden spoon, and add this liquid to the stockpot. Stir in the parsley, thyme, garlic, peppercorns, and salt, if using. Partially cover and simmer for at least 8 hours, adding water if needed to cover the ingredients.

Strain the stock into a large bowl or bowls, cover, and refrigerate overnight. Skim off the layer of fat on the surface and discard. Refrigerate or freeze the stock until needed.

*Fish stock is like court bouillon that is used to poach fish, except rather than cooking a whole fish in the liquid, you use the trimmings and bones from 2 to 3 lean white, non-oily fish. Store in the refrigerator for 3 to 4 days or freeze for 3 months.*

# FISH STOCK
*Makes about 2 quarts*

Combine the water, wine, vinegar, onions, carrots, celery, parsley, thyme, bay leaf, and salt in a large pot and bring to a boil. Add the fish, turn the heat down so the liquid is simmering, cover, and cook for 1 hour. Strain the stock through several layers of cheesecloth. Taste to adjust the seasonings and reduce the stock over high heat if needed.

1 ½ quarts water

2 cups dry white wine

⅓ cup white wine vinegar

2 medium unpeeled yellow onions, each stuck with 3 whole cloves

2 medium carrots, peeled and coarsely chopped

1 large stalk celery with leaves, coarsely chopped

3 sprigs flat-leaf parsley

1 sprig thyme

1 bay leaf

½ tablespoon salt

Trimmings and bones from 2 to 3 lean, white, non-oily fish

# CAST-IRON FAQs
## by David G. Smith

**What does it mean to season a pan?**

Seasoning is the process used to protect bare cast iron from rusting, provide a non-stick surface for cooking, and prevent food from interacting with the iron of the pan. The process oxidizes the iron to form magnetite, the black oxide of iron (as opposed to rust, the red oxide of iron). Seasoning is a three-step process: First, the cookware needs to be cleaned well to expose the bare metal (using oven cleaner or lye), applying a layer of vegetable or animal fat, and heating the cookware to bond the fat to the metal. Using the cookware continues to season it as foods deposit oils or fats on the pan.

**What happens to the fat? Can it get rancid?**

When the fats (vegetable or animal shortenings work best) are placed in the hot pan, it saturates the pan's surface. The heat after repeated uses gradually turns the fats to carbon creating the non stick surface—that's why seasoned pans are black. You need to make sure to wipe out the pan well, until it holds only a dull sheen. If you leave any melted fat on the pan, it can turn rancid over a period of time.

**Why can't I use detergent on my pan?**

Chemicals in detergents are designed to break down oils, so detergents will break down the very fats you want working for you.

**What if my pan is "pre-seasoned"?**

A pre-seasoned pan is sprayed with oil after it's manufactured, and baked at high temperatures to achieve iron oxidation. The oil seeps into the pores of the metal and the pan is ready to be used, although it's recommended that it should be re-seasoned. A pre-seasoned skillet is black, while an unseasoned skillet is silvery gray.

**Could my pan be coated with wax?**

Yes, an unseasoned new pan might be sold with a protective coating (wax or shellac). This coating must be removed (typically by scouring) to expose the bare cast iron surface before the pan is seasoned.

**Is it ever "too late" for a cast-iron pan?**

Unfortunately, yes. If the pan has a crack in it, or is rusted to the point where the surface is pitted—if the rust has actually eaten holes right through the cast iron—you won't be able to get these back to working condition.

# GLOSSARY

**al dente** usually referring to pasta or vegetables that are cooked until just tender yet retaining some "bite."

**baste** to moisten the surface of foods with a liquid or fat while cooking.

**blanch** to partially cook foods in boiling water to set the color, remove an outside skin (such as with nuts), or to soften the texture of vegetables. In many cases, vegetables are immediately plunged into cold water to stop the cooking and retain the color.

**boil** to cook food in rapidly bubbling liquid.

**braise** a moist-heat method of cooking foods in a covered pan, usually used with larger, tougher cuts of meat.

**broil** to cook foods under a direct heat source. (grilling is the same but the heat source is below the food.)

**broth/stock** the liquid derived from slowly simmering bones, herbs, and aromatic root vegetables in large quantities of water. The foundation for many dishes.

**chop** to cut into coarse, irregular pieces.

**deglaze** to stir a liquid into a hot pan that has been used for sautéing or roasting foods, thereby incorporating and dissolving the browned cooking solids that remain in the pan. A good source for pan sauces and juices.

**dice** to cut foods into small, uniform cubes.

**gratiné** to run food under a broiler to add additional color.

**julienne** to cut foods into thin, matchstick-like strips.

**mince** to chop finely.

**poach** to submerge foods in a gently simmering liquid.

**purée** to turn a solid food into a semi-liquid state.

**reduce** to boil a liquid to reduce the volume and concentrate flavors.

**refresh** to plunge hot food into cold water to arrest the cooking and set the color or to reconstitute, as with dried herbs.

**roast** a dry-heat method of cooking, usually in an uncovered, shallow pan.

**roux** equal parts by weight of flour and fat cooked together to create a thickening agent. It may be cooked to various stages from white to lightly colored to dark brown, depending on its final use.

**sauté** to cook foods quickly in a small amount of fat over high heat.

**simmer** the stage just below boil when bubbles just begin to break the surface.

**steam** to cook foods over rapidly boiling water in a covered pan.

**sweat** to soften vegetables in a minimum amount of fat in a covered pan over low heat.

**zest** (v.) to remove the colored outside layer of citrus fruit; (n.) the colorful outside layer of cit-

# ABOUT THE CONTRIBUTORS

JOANNA PRUESS is an award-winning author who has written extensively on food for the *New York Times Sunday Magazine,* the *Washington Post, Food Arts, Saveur, Food & Wine,* and the Associated Press syndicate. Her most recent cookbooks include *Mod Mex* and *Seduced by Bacon.*

Pruess is well-known in the specialty food business as a consultant, as well as a regular contributor to NASFT's *Specialty Food Magazine* and as a speaker at many shows. She has developed recipes for numerous clients including Bella Cucina Artful Food, Bigelow Tea, Stonewall Kitchen, Sarabeth's Kitchen, More Than Gourmet, Dufour Pastry Kitchens, and Vanns Spices. She founded and was the first director of the Cookingstudio, a cooking school within Kings Super Market in New Jersey, where she had more than 15,000 students in five years.

She and her husband, restaurant critic Bob Lape, reside in the Bronx, New York.

DAVID G. SMITH is a cofounder of the Wagner and Griswold Society, and coauthored *The Book of Griswold & Wagner* and *The Book of Wagner & Griswold.* He was a contributing author to the authoritative kitchenware book, *300 Years of Kitchen Collectibles,* and has had articles published in various antique trade publications. Smith, a judge in upstate New York, has collected cast iron for more than 30 years.

THE GRISWOLD MANUFACTURING COMPANY and THE WAGNER MANUFACTURING COMPANY, which were combined under the leadership of the Wagner brothers in the 1880s, first developed cast-iron, aluminum, and blended-metal cookware. These manufacturers remain a testimony to over a century of dedication to quality and value.

# INDEX